DISCOVERING THE JEWISH ROOTS OF THE LETTER OF

JAMES

BY DR. RIK WADGE

Part of the Discovering the Jewish Roots Commentary Series

Jewish Roots Publishing

www.discoveringthejewishroots.com

Scripture quotations marked MGI are taken from the Aramaic Peshitta New Testament Translation by Janet M. Magiera. Copyright @ 2006. Used by permission of Light of the Word Ministry Publishing.

Cover art by: Mason Williams and Sarah Richardson
Interior art design and editing by: Sarah Richardson

Printed in the United States of America
©2014 by Dr. Rik B. Wadge

Hardbound   ISBN # 978-0-692-27669-3
eBook   ISBN # 978-0-692-27670-9

Dedication

To family and friends who believed in this project.

Acknowledgements

I am so grateful to God for the opportunity to have written this book. It is my prayer that the reader finds as much excitement in the reading of this text as I have had in researching it. Many thanks to my congregation who journeyed with me through those months of exploration. We each found the Aramaic text to be richer than we had imagined. Special thanks to Janet Magiera for the primary translation used in this volume, and in whose wisdom and scholarship go far beyond her years.

May each of us find a deeper understanding for our lives as we seek Him through His Word!

Table of Contents

You'll explore the deeper meaning found only in the original Aramaic language.

Preface

Fifteen years after being ordained as a Southern Baptist pastor, my journey took me on a road that was to forever change my theological perspective. It was the summer of 2007, and I was doing preliminary research for a series I had been planning for my congregation. The subject which presented itself was the Holocaust that happened under Adolph Hitler. I was confronted with the fact that I knew very little about it. So, after having read many volumes on the subject, I decided that I needed to meet a survivor. When I realized that the scriptural understanding of these gentle souls was much more authentic than the westernized message I had been taught and had been teaching, a renewed commitment to find the authentic meaning of biblical phrases and idioms catapulted me into countless hours of study. And then, my research into the writings of the ancient rabbis led me to an unexpected discovery: The text of the New Testament can only be truly and correctly understood when read in the light of first-century Judaism!

Heretofore, according to my seminary training, I had studied Hebrew and Greek. It was the great Jewish historian Josephus who first made me realize the importance of the Aramaic (not Arabic) language. Imagine my shock when I realized that this language was spoken alongside Hebrew – it was even spoken by Yeshua (Jesus). While Hebrew was the language of the synagogue in the first-century Jewish community, Aramaic was the language of the people.

Though I'm certainly not an expert in the Aramaic language, I can state without reservation that my studies of Greek manuscripts had never unveiled the depth of meaning hidden in the Aramaic. I am indebted to the works of Janet Magiera, Rev. David Bauscher, George Lamsa, the early translations by James Murdock, and many others who have blazed the trail for modern studies in the Aramaic New Testament.

I must say that the Letter of James has literally come alive for me while in the process of writing this commentary. It has been many years in the making, and I pray that God will use something in this volume to touch the reader with the authentic message of this wonderful New Testament letter.

May you enjoy the journey as much as I have.

Dr. Rik B. Wadge

September 1st, 2014

Introduction

Jerusalem: 62 CE. A highly respected Jewish man between the ages of seventy and eighty years old was seen standing near the Temple. This was a place he could frequently be found. Wherever this man journeyed, a crowd of people would always gather around. He was both well known and well respected by both Orthodox Jews and those Jews who followed Rabbi Jesus.[1] This devout person was so revered that a certain sect of Jews living near the Dead Sea placed his teachings in their library alongside the other revered Jewish writings, including the Torah![2]

The famous historian, Josephus, tells us that this particular man was known by his contemporaries as "Ya'akov haTsadik," which translates as: *Jacob the Righteous*.[3] We know him as James.

Hegesippus, who lived immediately after the time of the Apostles, tells us that Jacob[4] or Ya'akov was a pious man who kept the Nazarite vows and regularly practiced fasting. It is told of him that he put such little priority on bathing that he bathed only as it pertained to his religious standing before God. In other words, he only bathed in the mikvah.[5]

A fourth-century church father and historian, Eusebius, records that Ya'akov was known for his many prayers. In fact, he was known for praying so often that his knees had grown overly callused. For this he

---

1 Though the name "Jesus" is what most people know the Savior by today, in the first-century they would have known Him by His Hebrew name: Yeshua. For an in-depth study on the name "Yeshua" see "Discovering the Jewish Roots of Matthew."

2 This Jewish sect mentioned were the Essenes. See Risto Santala, The Messiah in the New Testament in the Light of Rabbinical Writings.

3 See Josephus's account of James in Antiquities of the Jews, Book 20, chapter 9.

4 About the name Jacob: Our common translation (James) is actually a Latin transliteration, which comes from the Greek (Jacob), which comes from the Hebrew (Ya'akov).

5 A "mikvah" was a type of ancient baptismal used by the Jewish people for ceremonial washing before certain religious duties.

was nicknamed, "Camel-Knees."

It is recorded that on one particular day when the crowds had gathered around, some religious leaders approached the elderly sage. Ya'akov was busy telling the people about Jesus (Yeshua), the Messiah. These men suggested that Ya'akov go up to the top of the temple wall to teach so that the entire crowd might better be able to hear him speak. However, upon arriving at the top, the religious leaders pushed the winded old man off the edge of the wall in an attempt to kill him. The elderly man lay crumpled at the base of the temple wall, yet alive.

They then proceeded to take up rocks and stoned him as he lay there. Before he died, (as had his half-brother, Yeshua), Ya'akov asked God to forgive them for what they were doing. That was to be his final prayer. Upon hearing him, one of the men in the crowd finished him off by striking him across the head with a club.

That is the story of Ya'akov Ben Yosef. And this was the last day of his life...

Chapter 1

The Letter of Ya'akov (James)

Ya'akov was named for one of the three great patriarchs of Judaism. And he was thrown down from approximately the same spot where Yeshua had been tempted. Where the devil had failed to tempt the Messiah, he now had a minor victory by tempting the religious leaders to murder Ya'akov. Tradition tells us that this particular corner of the wall was called "The Place of Trumpeting." It was the location at the top of the temple from which the shofar (a hebrew trumpet made from a ram's horn) was blown. As a matter of fact, it was from this very place that the long-awaited Messiah should be heralded upon His arrival![6]

Alfred Edersheim in his third book on the life of Yeshua gives us a great example of this connection among the writings of the sages. He writes,

> Our Rabbis give this tradition: In the hour when King Messiah cometh, He standeth upon the roof of the Sanctuary, and proclaims to Israel, saying, Ye poor suffering, the time of your redemption draweth nigh. And if ye believe, rejoice in My Light, which is risen upon you... Isa_60:1... upon you only... Isa_60:2... In that hour will the Holy One, blessed be His Name, make the Light of the Messiah and of Israel to shine forth; and all shall come to the Light of the King Messiah and of Israel, as it is written... Isa_60:3... And they shall come and lick the dust from under the feet of the King Messiah, as it is written, Isa_49:23... And all shall come and fall on their faces before the Messiah and before Israel, and say, We will be servants to Him and to Israel.

---

6   Jewish tradition holds that the highest point of the temple and the appearance of the Messiah are directly connected.

And every one in Israel shall have 2,800 servants, as it is written, Zec_8:23.[7]

Well back to our story, it seems the Messiah's half-brother was busy proclaiming His arrival – from this very spot – on the last day of his life.

As I think through the events that transpired, I wonder how it was that Ya'akov went from being a dispassionate unbeliever, to become a most impassioned follower? Just what was the catalyst for the dramatic change? What would turn a devout Jew from scoffer, into the very first leader of *The Way* later to be called *Christians*.

Let's take a journey together and see if we might find answers to these questions. Are you willing? Then let's get started!

First of all, very little is known about the family and home life of Ya'akov Ben Yosef.[8] Nevertheless, with the help of some ancient traditions and a handful of scripture references, I believe we will be able to view a basic picture of the household of Yosef.[9]

Let's begin with a great story that was told all throughout ancient Christendom which, although apocryphal, may help to give us an understanding of this biblical character known as Ya'akov, and the letter that bears his name.

This document comes down to us under the simple name, "The history of Joseph the Carpenter."

> There was a man whose name was Joseph, sprung from a family of Bethlehem, a town of Judah, and the city of King David. This same man, being well furnished with wisdom and learning, was made a priest in the temple of the Lord. He was, besides, skillful

---

7   Edersheim, The Life and Times of Jesus the Messiah, Book 3, chapter 1
8   James, the son of Joseph.
9   The name "Yosef" is translated today as "Joseph," as in Joseph and Mary.

5

in his trade, which was that of a carpenter; and after the manner of all men, he married a wife. Moreover, he begot for himself sons and daughters, four sons, namely, and two daughters. Now these are their names – Judas, Justus, James, and Simon. The names of the two daughters were Assia and Lydia. At length the wife of righteous Joseph, a woman intent on the divine glory in all her works, departed this life. But Joseph, that righteous man, my father after the flesh, and the spouse of my mother Mary, went away with his sons to his trade, practicing the art of a carpenter.   3. Now when righteous Joseph became a widower, my mother Mary, blessed, holy, and pure, was already twelve years old. For her parents offered her in the temple when she was three years of age, and she remained in the temple of the Lord nine years. Then when the priests saw that the virgin, holy and God-fearing, was growing up, they spoke to each other, saying, "Let us search out a man, righteous and pious, to whom Mary may be entrusted until the time of her marriage; lest, if she remain in the temple, it happen to her as is wont to happen to women, and lest on that account we sin, and God be angry with us."   4. Therefore they immediately sent out, and assembled twelve old men of the tribe of Judah. And they wrote down the names of the twelve tribes of Israel. And the lot fell upon the pious old man, righteous Joseph. Then the priests answered, and said to my blessed mother, "Go with Joseph, and be with him till the time of your marriage." Righteous Joseph therefore received my mother, and led her away to his own house. [10]

As with most oral tradition – whether about George Washington, or about one's own great-grandparent – one must sift through the material, separating that which has come to us as a result of an older tradition, from that which is fanciful verbiage for the purpose of good storytelling.

According to tradition, Miryam (Mary) was twelve years old when Yosef's (Joseph's) wife died, and fourteen when she was married.[11] As

---

10 Schaff, Anti-Nicene Fathers Vol 8, "the History of Joseph the Carpenter" pg. 389.
11 Kiddushin (tosafot) 41a

girls from this time period would normally have had their Bat Mitzvah[12] at the age of twelve, and being from a devout family, she would most certainly have been Bat Mitzvah'd prior to her marriage.

It was the custom at that time for boys to be Bar Mitzvah'd at the age of thirteen. Yet, we see the gospels put Yeshua (Jesus) at the temple with the Rabbis at the age of twelve. And remember, they were amazed at His learning.[13] This probably means He was testing with the rabbis for his Bar Mitzvah. (Although rare, it was the custom that a boy could be Bar Mitzvah'd younger than thirteen if the rabbis considered him to be mature). By pointing out His age, Luke is showing that Yeshua was unnaturally wise beyond His tender years.

For Miryam (Mary), being Bat Mitzvah'd meant that she would now be considered as *a daughter of the covenant* and now responsible to keep the commandments of God. (Later, this fact will play a dramatic role in our understanding of the enormous implications of her alleged fornication which resulted in her Son, Yeshua).

An interesting side-note: first-century Jewish tradition considered unmarried females over the age of twenty to be cursed by God.[14] Although we don't rely on oral traditions, they do normally grow out of some element of truth. And this situation from the gospels lends credence to the story. It also gives us uncanny insight into the family structure.

> **Mark 8:22-26** As they came to Bethsaida, some people brought a blind man to Jesus. They begged Jesus to touch him. 23 Jesus took the blind man's hand and led him out of the village. He spit into the man's eyes and placed his hands on him.

---

12 "Bat Mitzvah" literally means: "Daughter of the Commandment." This was/is a Jewish ceremony where a young girl is brought before the congregation and recognized as being part of the religious community and thereby bears responsibility for keeping the commands of God.

13 See Luke 2:47

14 Kiddushin 29b

Jesus asked him, "*Can you see anything?*" 24 The man looked up and said, "*I see people. They look like trees walking around.*" 25 Then Jesus placed his hands on the man's eyes a second time, and the man saw clearly. His sight was normal again. He could see everything clearly even at a distance. 26 Jesus told him when he sent him home, "Don't go into the village."

It seems a bit strange that Yeshua heals a blind man by spitting in his eyes. Yet, in this example, Yeshua will use the writings of the Talmud (still oral tradition at that time) to prove that He is the Messiah.

This is the teaching which Rabbi Yeshua alludes to when healing the man with spittle.

> A man once came before a Rabbi and said to him, "I am sure that this man is the firstborn." The Rabbi asked, "How is it that you are certain of this?" The man said, "Because when [sick] people came to his father he would tell them 'Go to my son. He is firstborn and his spittle heals.'" Might he not have been the firstborn of his mother [and not of his father]? [No, because] there is a tradition that the spittle of the firstborn of a father heals, but that of the firstborn of a mother does not heal.
> - (Bava Batra 126b)

The Jewish Talmud states that the firstborn son of a father can bring healing to the eyes by using his spittle, but the firstborn son of a mother cannot.

Yeshua obviously knew this tradition and purposely chose this particular method of healing in order to make a point.

In "The History of Joseph the Carpenter," we learned that Yosef was a widower. He had several children from this first wife, who were the brothers and sisters of the Lord mentioned in the gospels.[15] Yeshua was

---

15 Cp. Matthew 13:55, "Isn't he the carpenter's son? Isn't his mother called Miryam?

Miryam's firstborn, of course, since she was a virgin when the Holy Spirit came upon her. Actually, that Miryam had no other children before Yeshua was undisputed even at that time. It was also well known that Yosef had already fathered children with his first wife. Therefore, Yeshua could not possibly be the firstborn son of Yosef.

The Talmud states that a firstborn son of a mother cannot bring healing, but, by using his spittle, the firstborn son of a father can bring healing. Yeshua, being the firstborn Son of a mother, in fact, brought healing to the blind man's eyes. Therefore, either the Rabbis were wrong and their traditions were incorrect, or they must face the fact that Yeshua *was* the firstborn son of a father, but not of Yosef. He was the firstborn son of another father... His Heavenly Father!

In order for this healing to make sense and carry it's full impact, we're forced to see two things:

1. Yeshua was using a rabbinic tradition in order to show that He was the Son of God and the long-awaited Messiah.

2. Yosef had older children, and Miryam was their step-mother.

This little story is going to help us better understand the dynamics of the household of Yeshua the Messiah, and of the Lord's half-brothers: Ya'akov (James), the author of the letter we're studying now, and Yehudah (Jude), the author of the New Testament letter which bears his name.

Here's our story. In this scenario, Yosef is betrothed to Miryam. For them, this beginning period which we know as *the engagement* is called *erusin* or *kiddushin,* both terms meaning sanctification. There would have been some type of public ceremony which the local townsfolk would have attended and witnessed. Let's just say it is highly probable that most everyone in that little community were aware that these two were promised to each other.

It was customary that this period of kiddushin was to last about a year. Afterward, it would be followed by the *nissu'un* or *chupah*, which is the actual ceremony of marriage. It is here that the couple is considered to be legally married and are then allowed to live under the same roof. Once kiddushin has been entered into, the laws of adultery apply.

So here we are. Miryam is at the age of accountability, and is considered a young adult. She's participated in a public ceremony at which she's pledged herself to Yosef alone. But then, before they are legally joined in marriage under the chupah, Miryam finds she is expecting a child. The gospels are spot-on-accurate in their description of the couples' desperate situation.

(Think about the betrothal of Yeshua to His bride. We, too, are waiting to live together under the same roof with our beloved. We, too, are called to be faithful to Him, and Him alone).

Now, ponder this situation between Yosef and Miryam.

Yosef is an older gentleman who's been married once before with six children: four boys and two girls. He's lost his wife prematurely, and the children have lost their mother. He now becomes engaged to a young girl who has just come of age. It's even probable that his betrothed is younger than some of his children.

Think about the family dynamics here! Imagine how difficult it might be for these children to accept Miryam into their home, into their life. Now, add the fact that dear old dad is going to marry a girl who, it seems, has already broken her vows and been unfaithful to him. Yet, Yosef had a dream in which an angel instructed him to go through with the wedding. How easy do you think it would have been for the children of Yosef to believe their father's explanation? With children and especially teenagers, nothing is easy. But for these kids it must have seemed impossible.

At that time, according to tradition, Yeshua was born as the seventh child of Yosef – the seventh son – representing perfection. How much resentment might there have been between Yosef's children and this new baby? And now the entire family is uprooted from their home, their friends, and their family, because their parents believed this child to somehow be the long-awaited Messiah. According to tradition, because of King Herod's paranoia, Yosef and his family were shuffled back-and-forth between the small Jewish communities and synagogues of Alexandria, Egypt, in order to keep the child safe. At that time, there was a strong Jewish community in Egypt. However, it was still Egypt – the diaspora – and couldn't be compared to living in *the land* (haAretz). Even today, most Jews avoid visiting Egypt altogether.

Man! Think about it. Of all places, the family moved to the very spot in which the Jews had been enslaved for so long... the very place from which God rescued them through Moses... the same place they spoke about each year at Passover!

It's pretty clear from later results that resentment was probably brewing in the hearts of Yeshua's siblings.

Now, in order for Yosef to have been a responsible father to young Yeshua, he would have had to fulfill several requirements. These requirements are laid out for us in the Babylonian Talmud.

> The father is required to circumcise his son; to redeem him [referring to the first-born son, as per the Biblical passages in Numbers 18: 15-16]; to teach him Torah; to assure that he marries; and to teach him a trade. Some say he must also teach him to swim. Rabbi Judah says, "Whoever does not teach his son a trade teaches him robbery."
> -(Babylonian Talmud, Tractate Kiddushin, p. 29a)

- Yosef would have been present for the Brit Milah (circumcision).
- Yosef would have been the one given the task of teaching Yeshua

the five books of Moses (i.e. Torah).

- Yosef, however, wasn't around to see Yeshua marry. In fact, the final stage of the Messiah's betrothal and marriage will take place in the future at what's called the "Wedding Supper of the Lamb." This is where Jew and gentile are to wed the Bridegroom. This is why He said, "I go to prepare a place for you." Now is the time of betrothal where the gentiles have their opportunity to come into the matrimonial relationship.

- Yosef taught Yeshua a trade.

- But, instead of Yosef teaching Yeshua to swim…
  His Heavenly Father taught Him to walk on water!

Fast forward. It's now about the year 3768 on the Jewish calendar (about 8 CE), and Yeshua is twelve years old and is standing before the rabbis at the temple in Jerusalem in preparation for His Bar Mitzvah. Fast forward a little further. Yeshua is a man of thirty years (the minimal age for a man to become a rabbi), and has left home to gather followers. It's impossible to nail down the chain of events exactly, but right about the time that Yeshua begins His public ministry, Yosef dies. This timing lines up with oral tradition, and there are hints of it in the gospels. Let me show you.

> **Matthew 13:55-57 ESV** "Is not this the carpenter's son? Is not his mother called Mary? And are not his brothers James and Joseph and Simon and Judas? (56) And are not all his sisters with us? Where then did this man get all these things?" (57) And they took offense at him. But Jesus said to them, "A prophet is not without honor except in his hometown and in his own household."

Here we see the source of the oral traditions regarding the brothers and sisters in Yeshua's household. Ya'akov is mentioned first, indicating that he was the eldest son. Yehudah (Judah), is also mentioned. We typically know him as Jude, but in this particular translation his name is translated as Judas. We see that His mother, Miryam is present, but there is no mention of Yosef. Notice the timing on the statement that Yeshua makes as he quotes the proverb:

> *"A prophet is not without honor except in his hometown and in his own household."*

His usage of this proverb tells us unmistakably that Yeshua's family was, at best, fractured over His calling. To say, "I'm without honor in my own home," is a powerful statement regarding His family. Yeshua was explaining that most of His family didn't believe that He was the Anointed One!"

Mark's gospel tells that the crowds were so thick around Yeshua one day that He and his disciples couldn't even eat. Notice how His family reacts to this.

> **Mark 3:21 ESV**   And when His family heard it, they went out to seize Him, for they were saying, "He is out of his mind."

What an embarrassment! He's lost his marbles! He's one french fry shy of a Happy Meal!

In his gospel, John writes:

> **John 7:5 ESV**   For not even His brothers believed in Him.

At the crucifixion, who is it that we see standing at the foot of the cross? His brothers? His sisters?

> **John 19:25 ESV**   ...but standing by the cross of Jesus were His mother and His mother's sister, Mary the wife of Clopas, and Mary Magdalene.

His siblings weren't present during the most horrific day of His life. Only his mother and a few friends stood by His side. Something else is evident here.

John 19:26-27 ESV When Jesus saw his mother and the disciple whom He loved standing nearby, He said to His mother, "Woman, behold, your son!" (27) Then He said to the disciple, "Behold, your mother!" And from that hour the disciple took her to his own home.

Jewish law requires children to *honor* their father and mother. This honoring includes caring for them in their later years. Yosef is absent from the scene, long since passed away. But where are all of the step-children, Yeshua's brothers and sisters? They are nowhere to be seen. In this event, to whom does Yeshua entrust the care of His mother? He places her care into the hands of "the disciple whom Jesus loved," a non-blood relative, John (Yochanon). Why? Obviously, Miryam was never fully accepted into Yosef's household by his children. Had they actually considered her family, Yeshua would never had the need to call on a non-family member to care for her.

Those are the family dynamics in the life of Yeshua. That is the attitude of Ya'akov, the man who would one day become head over all the believers in Jerusalem following the death and resurrection of the Messiah.

Next, we journey into the letter which is considered to be the most Jewish of all writings in the New Testament! But first we must set the scene properly.

Acts 1:1-14 ESV In the first book, O Theophilus, I have dealt with all that Jesus began to do and teach, (2) until the day when He was taken up, after He had given commands through the Holy Spirit to the apostles whom He had chosen. (3) He presented Himself alive to them after His suffering by many proofs, appearing to them during forty days and speaking about the kingdom of God. (4) And while staying with them He ordered them not to depart from Jerusalem, but to wait for the promise of the Father, which, He said, "you heard from me; (5) for John baptized with water, but you will be baptized with the

Holy Spirit not many days from now." (6) So when they had come together, they asked Him, "Lord, will you at this time restore the kingdom to Israel?" (7) He said to them, "It is not for you to know times or seasons that the Father has fixed by His own authority. (8) But you will receive power when the Holy Spirit has come upon you, and you will be my witnesses in Jerusalem and in all Judea and Samaria, and to the end of the earth." (9) And when He had said these things, as they were looking on, He was lifted up, and a cloud took Him out of their sight. (10) And while they were gazing into heaven as He went, behold, two men stood by them in white robes, (11) and said, "Men of Galilee, why do you stand looking into heaven? This Jesus, who was taken up from you into heaven, will come in the same way as you saw Him go into heaven." (12) Then they returned to Jerusalem from the mount called Olives, which is near Jerusalem, a Sabbath day's journey away. (13) And when they had entered, they went up to the upper room, where they were staying, Peter and John and James and Andrew, Philip and Thomas, Bartholomew and Matthew, James the son of Alphaeus and Simon the Zealot and Judas the son of James. (14) All these with one accord were devoting themselves to prayer, together with the women and Mary the mother of Jesus, *and his brothers.*

Excuse me, but would you kindly repeat that last sentence?

*"All these with one accord were devoting themselves to prayer, together with the women and Mary the mother of Jesus, **and his brothers.**"*

That's brothers. Plural. Just what happened in the hearts of Yeshua's brothers between that dreadful day at the crucifixion and this day in the upper room? What could cause such a great change in a period of less than two months?[16] Rabbi Sha'ul of Tarsus[17] gives the us the account in his first letter to the assembly at Corinth.

---

16 Yeshua had been seen for some 40 days leaving 10 days remaining before the Feast of Shavuot and the giving of the Spirit.

17 Today, we usually translate the Hebrew name "Sha'ul" as "Saul."

1 Corinthians 15:1-8 ESV   Now I would remind you, brothers, of the gospel I preached to you, which you received, in which you stand, (2) and by which you are being saved, if you hold fast to the word I preached to you - unless you believed in vain. (3) For I delivered to you as of first importance what I also received: that Christ died for our sins in accordance with the Scriptures, (4) that He was buried, that He was raised on the third day in accordance with the Scriptures, (5) and that He appeared to Cephas, then to the twelve. (6) Then He appeared to more than five hundred brothers at one time, most of whom are still alive, though some have fallen asleep. (7) *Then He appeared to James,* then to all the apostles. (8) Last of all, as to one untimely born, He appeared also to me.

Clearly, the event that caused Ya'akov to believe was the resurrection.

One of the strongest proofs for the Messiah's resurrection is the fact that so many who didn't believe before, did afterward. Think about it: the brother that all of Jerusalem saw crucified, dead, and buried is now having a conversation with you – in the flesh! Something like that would most definitely change a person's life! And it did.

As a result of this power-encounter with Yeshua, Ya'akov and Yehudah become a part of the believing community, which included their step-mother, Miryam (Mary). This is the first time we see Ya'akov and Miryam together. Not only together, but together in prayer! Just what had the fact of the resurrection done to this family? It brought them all together. Can you imagine the conversations which must have taken place between the grown children of Yosef and their step-mother, the apologies, the tears, the rejoicing?

Somewhere between the years 37-40 CE,[18] we know that Ya'akov is in

18 I.S.B.E. under the article entitled "James" which dates Paul's visit between the years 37-38; Whereas others estimate that this event took place after the death of King Aretas in 40CE. It's obvious that whatever the date of this meeting, it happens shortly after Paul's life-changing encounter on the Road to Damascus

Jerusalem, because Rabbi Sha'ul visits with him there.

> **Galatians 1:18-19 ESV**   Then after three years I went up to Jerusalem to visit Cephas and remained with him fifteen days. (19) But I saw none of the other apostles except James the Lord's brother.

It's interesting to note that Rabbi Sha'ul meets with the Lord's brother shortly after his encounter with the risen Savior on the road to Damascus. Why? Because, like Sha'ul, Ya'akov was known to have been an ultra-orthodox Jew (by today's standards), and is now not only a believer in the resurrected Yeshua, but is looked to as the leader of this new Jewish movement.

It is here we begin to see a desire among the followers to report to Ya'akov. When Kefa (Peter) was freed from prison with the help of angelic powers, he said this:

> **Acts 12:17 ESV**   But motioning to them with his hand to be silent, he described to them how the Lord had brought him out of the prison. And he said, "Tell these things to James and to the brothers." Then he departed and went to another place.

By the way, just where was the physical location where Ya'akov's authority was respected? In Jerusalem! The Jerusalem congregation was considered the center of this new Jewish movement. This is true, in part, because it was to Jerusalem that the Messiah would one day return and from Jerusalem that He would one day reign.

Tradition tells us that Ya'akov was considered the first leader of the movement in Jerusalem.[19] We find the first mention of this in Eusebius' History, Book 2:

> Then James, whom the ancients surnamed The Just, on account

---

around 37CE.
19 Eusebius' Ecclesiastical History, Book II. Ch 1. 2, 3

of the excellence of his virtue, is recorded to have been the first to be made bishop of the church of Jerusalem. This James was called the brother of the Lord because he was known as a son of Joseph, and Joseph was supposed to be the father of Christ, because the Virgin, being betrothed to him, was found with child by the Holy Ghost before they came together, "Mat_1:18" as the account of the holy Gospels shows. 3. But Clement in the sixth book of his Hypotyposes writes thus: "For they say that Peter and James and John after the ascension of our Saviour, as if also preferred by our Lord, strove not after honor, but chose James the Just bishop of Jerusalem."

So, Peter, James, and John, or more properly, Kefa, Ya'akov, and Yochanon (the "Sons of Thunder," and Yeshua's closest disciples), put into practice what their Master had taught them. These three did not become the main leaders but chose the Lord's brother, Ya'akov, instead. This demonstration of humility is a far cry from where their hearts had been only a short time before as the immature, self-promoting disciples we read about in the gospels!

Did you happen to notice Eusebius' superimposition of the title "bishop" onto Ya'akov? Bishop is not a title which would have been used in first-century Judaism. It would, however, become a normal expression of authority in Eusebius' fourth-century life.

In addition, the idea of Ya'akov presiding over a *church in Jerusalem* is another anachronistic projection. There was no such thing as a church in Jerusalem at that time. The term church comes from the Greek term "ekklesia" which means "an assembly." An assembly, on the other hand, is something the Jews in first-century Jerusalem would definitely have known. Their word for it was "kahal." It's easy to see how so many today are misled and find a complete separation between the cultures of the old and new testaments through the faulty and inaccurate terms that were derived centuries later by individuals who were far removed from the influence of the Jewish culture.

We have an example of Ya'akov's leadership abilities recorded for us in the book of Acts which involves the question of the Gentiles. The year is somewhere around 51 CE. Sha'ul (Paul) and Bar-Nabba (Barnabus) have come before the apostles and elders in Jerusalem to seek clarification for the inclusion of the gentiles into the assemblies. Should they be circumcised or not? Here's part of the discussion.

> **Acts 15:12-22 ESV** And all the assembly fell silent, and they listened to Barnabas and Paul as they related what signs and wonders God had done through them among the Gentiles. (13) After they finished speaking, James replied, "Brothers, listen to me. (14) Simeon has related how God first visited the Gentiles, to take from them a people for his name. (15) And with this the words of the prophets agree, just as it is written, (16) 'After this I will return, and I will rebuild the tent of David that has fallen; I will rebuild its ruins, and I will restore it, (17) that the remnant of mankind may seek the Lord, and all the Gentiles who are called by my name, says the Lord, who makes these things (18) known from of old.' (19) Therefore my judgment is that we should not trouble those of the Gentiles who turn to God, (20) but should write to them to abstain from the things polluted by idols, and from sexual immorality, and from what has been strangled, and from blood. (21) For from ancient generations Moses has had in every city those who proclaim him, for he is read every Sabbath in the synagogues." (22) Then it seemed good to the apostles and the elders, with the whole church, to choose men from among them and send them to Antioch with Paul and Barnabas. They sent Judas called Barsabbas, and Silas, leading men among the brothers...

According to Ya'akov's wisdom, the Gentiles would learn naturally how to be disciples by learning from the teachings of Moses (the Torah). It was presumed that these new gentile believers in the Jewish Messiah would naturally join them in the synagogues each week and would hear God's instructions being taught!

Also in the book of Acts (which was written some twenty years after Sha'ul's first meeting with Ya'akov), Rabbi Sha'ul is giving a report about his third missionary journey. And guess what? Ya'akov is *still* the head of the council at Jerusalem! Why would this be? Ya'akov was known to be a righteous man. Remember that he was called, "Ya'akov haTzadik" ("James the Just")! In fact, Jerome tells us that Ya'akov held the position of leadership in the Jerusalem congregation for some thirty years.[20]

The book of Acts gives us a glimpse of this man's incredible heart and wisdom.

> **Acts 21:17-25 ESV** When we had come to Jerusalem, the brothers received us gladly. (18) On the following day Paul went in with us to James, and all the elders were present. (19) After greeting them, he related one by one the things that God had done among the Gentiles through his ministry. (20) And when they heard it, they glorified God. And they said to him, "You see, brother, how many thousands there are among the Jews of those who have believed. They are all zealous for the law, (21) and they have been told about you that you teach all the Jews who are among the Gentiles to forsake Moses, telling them not to circumcise their children or walk according to our customs. (22) What then is to be done? They will certainly hear that you have come. (23) Do therefore what we tell you. We have four men who are under a vow; (24) take these men and purify yourself along with them and pay their expenses, so that they may shave their heads. Thus all will know that there is nothing in what they have been told about you, but that you yourself also live in observance of the law. (25) But as for the Gentiles who have believed, we have sent a letter with our judgment that they should abstain from what has been sacrificed to idols, and from blood, and from what has been strangled, and from sexual immorality."

---

20 Jerome, On Illustrious men, 2

It's here that Ya'akov tells Rabbi Sha'ul he should convince his critics that he's still faithfully keeping the Torah. For this reason, Sha'ul took the Nazarite vow and even paid the fee for four other men to do so as well. (*If only he could convince Christians today that Sha'ul never stopped keeping the Torah. Oy vey!*)

Remember the words of Yeshua:

> **Matthew 5:19 CJB** So whoever disobeys the least of these mitzvot and teaches others to do so will be called the least in the Kingdom of Heaven. But whoever obeys them and so teaches will be called great in the Kingdom of Heaven.

It was a mere four years after Sha'ul's meeting with him that Ya'akov would be pushed from the top of the walls of Jerusalem, be stoned, beaten, and buried. This is all that we know concerning the life of Ya'akov. Let us now study all that remains of what this great man has written.

The International Standard Bible Encyclopedia states:

> *"The Epistle of James is the most Jewish writing in the New Testament."*[21]

Regarding the date, we can deduce when this letter was written by three pieces of evidence:

1. Eusebius records that some blamed the fall of Jerusalem in 70CE directly on Ya'akov's death.[22] So, his martyrdom took place before that.
2. Ya'akov is martyred in 62CE, so obviously, the letter had been written prior to that date.
3. The papyrus scraps found in the caves of Qumran date from somewhere between 50-60CE.

---

21 I.S.B.E. "James, the Lord's brother"
22 Eusebius' Ecclesiastical History 2.23

The letter itself is written completely from a Jewish perspective. Knowing that Ya'akov served in Jerusalem helps us to pin-point the location where the letter was written, but honestly, we would have probably come to that same conclusion through the many allusions to it used in the letter itself *(images of the nearby sea, ships, figs, oil, wine, bitter springs; and a well-known Jewish phrase from that area, "the former and later rain").*

In the letter there are no less than thirty-four references to the teachings of Yeshua HaMashiach, the Jewish Messiah, from the Sermon on the Mount. In addition, the entire letter is addressed specifically to Jewish readers. Make no mistake: this is a letter written to Jews by a Jew!

> **James 1:1 MGI** James, a servant of God and of our Lord Jesus Christ, to the twelve tribes that are scattered among the nations: Peace.

Make a note that neither Ya'akov nor Yehudah ever call themselves Yeshua's brothers. Both refer to themselves as His servants.

In addition to having being named after the great patriarch, and as Jewish tradition prescribes, being his first son, Ya'akov is named after his grandfather, Ya'akov, Yosef's father. The following scripture lends further credence to the idea that Ya'akov is Yosef's first son.

> **Matthew 1:16 CJB** Ya'akov was the father of Yosef, the husband of Miryam, from whom was born the Yeshua who was called the Messiah.

Next, we see that Ya'akov calls the Messiah by a very special name: MarYah! This Aramaic term is only used to designate the Hebrew YHVH from the TaNaK (Old Testament). MarYah is the term used as a respectful substitute for the Unpronounceable Name some sixty-five hundred times! By referring to Yeshua by the Divine Name, Ya'akov makes it extremely clear right at the onset that he considers the Messiah to be none other than God Himself! Perhaps one of the reasons he did may be the conversation he had with Yeshua after He rose from the dead! Secondly, he did because the scriptures demand it.

Speaking through the prophet Isaiah, YHVH clearly proclaims:

> **Isaiah 43:11 NIV** I, even I, am the LORD, and apart from me there is no savior.

Most likely, you know him as 'John the Baptizer,' but just what was the purpose for Yochanon the Immerser's ministry?

> **Matthew 3:1-3 NIV** In those days John the Baptist came, preaching in the Desert of Judea (2) and saying, "Repent, for the kingdom of heaven is near." (3) "This is He who was spoken of through the prophet Isaiah: 'A voice of one calling in the desert, Prepare the way for the Lord, make straight paths for Him.' "

That is a quotation from Isaiah 40:3. In the Isaiah passage, we find "YHVH" where our English translation has "the Lord." The Greek word for Lord, "kurios," is quite generic and can even mean simply "land-owner." John, however, was to prepare the way for YHVH.

Now look at the Matthew passage as translated from the original Aramaic:

> **Matthew 3:2-3 Murdock** and said: Repent; the kingdom of heaven hath approached. (3) For this is He of whom it was said, by Isaiah the prophet: The voice of one crying in the wilderness, Prepare ye the way of the Lord (MarYah), make smooth His paths.

In the very first sentence of his letter, Ya'akov boldly declares to whom it is that he belongs: (*MarYah; The Lord Yah; YHVH!*) he is the servant of the Most High God, who is also the Messiah!

23

Ya'akov addresses his letter of instruction to:

"the twelve tribes dispersed among the peoples."[23]

To all the sons of Israel and to each of the tribes. This is a letter to all of the Jews of the day, and because of Ya'akov's good reputation, they all took heed.

The "diaspora" was considered to extend all the way from Rome to Babylon. Basically, anything outside of "the land," any place where the Jews were scattered due to persecution or unrest, was considered the diaspora (including Egypt, Greece, Philistia, etc.).

The Greek term "diaspora" is used to translate the Aramaic word "d'azriy-an," which means: "to sow"[24] *(as in: God has sown His people among the gentiles)*. The word is listed as a passive participle in the Peshitta text, meaning that the scattering of the Jews was outside of their control. It's as if God scattered the seeds of His people throughout the known world in order to influence and prepare the Gentiles for the message of the One True God and of His Messiah. Actually, this is exactly what happened. This Jewish message concerning the need for redemption – for the sacrifice of a perfect lamb in order to take away the sins of the whole world – permeated the pagan world like seed being sown into a dying crop. And today, that message is still being sewn and bearing fruit. People everywhere are hearing about the hope of a Kingdom which waits just over the horizon, and about a God that invites both Jew and Gentile to come and live!

The miraculous transformation that God brings within a person, a family, or even a society is expressed in the simple greeting in Ya'akov's very first sentence: Shalom (Peace)!

The Aramaic actually has "Sh'lam," but we're probably better acquainted

---

23 James 1:1 Translation used here is from the Aramaic English New Testament, Roth
24 SEDRA3 ܗܙܪܥ "to sow." See Jenning's Lexicon, pg 67; Smith's Syriac Dictionary has "scattered seed." pg. 121

with it's Hebrew counterpart, "Shalom." This word is used in numerous places in the scriptures, but the one that comes to my mind first is where Rabbi Yeshua uses it in the Sermon on the Mount:

> **Matthew 5:9** Murdock Blessed are the cultivators of peace: for they shall be called sons of God!

Just what is God's concept of a person who pursues shalom, one who is a peacemaker? What a great question! And it's a question that fits perfectly with the scope of one of my interests: Paleo-Hebrew origins.

There is one person in the scriptures who is specifically called a peacemaker. He is found in a story from the book of Numbers. The story is about a man named Pinchas, who was the grandson of Aaron. Just what did Pinchas do to earn the title "Peacemaker" from God? If you recall, he took a spear and ran it through a man and woman who were fornicating. It is for this specific action, the killing of these two people, that God considered him a peacemaker (Numbers 25:6-13). Pinchas later became the High Priest of Israel!

The definition of peace is: "to be made whole."[25] Peace does not necessarily have anything to do with being calm or passive, as we might think of it. Peace (shalom) may even be active, as indicated by it's Paleo-Hebrew form.[26]

W Sheen ש	ל Lamed ל	ו Vav ו	מ Mem ם
teeth	cattle goad	nail, hook	water
destroy	authority	secure	chaos

We might render this four-letter pictoral designation for Shalom as: "To

---

25 Jeff Benner's Ancient Hebrew Lexicon of the Bible, #2845 "shalom" "to be in a state of wholeness." pg.459

26 Dr. Frank T. Seekins, Hebrew Word Pictures, pg. 94

destroy the authority that secures Chaos."

So we see that shalom is brought about by activism, rather than pacifism. Yeshua is the Prince of Peace. He gained that title by actively destroying the authority that brought chaos to the world by crucifying the power of sin on the cross. This same Rabbi said we are to "pursue being a peacemaker."

"Blessed are" is a present state of being and a lifestyle choice. We actively pursue peace by destroying chaos. Chaos indicates "imbalanced living as a fractured individual," whereas shalom indicates "balance, wholeness, spiritual well-being."

No wonder God sowed His message of how to find peace into a world that desperately needs to find it.

Chapter 2

James 1:1 MGI   James, a servant of God and of our Lord Jesus Christ, to the twelve tribes that are scattered among the nations: Peace.

The Jews had been dispersed throughout the land outside of Israel due to various persecutions throughout the ages. This new sect of Judaism was no exception, however, they were being persecuted by their own brothers because of their faith in Yeshua.

Acts 8:1 ESV   And Saul approved of his execution. And there arose on that day a great persecution against the church in Jerusalem, and they were all scattered throughout the regions of Judea and Samaria, except the apostles.

After the death of Stephen, Sha'ul was a rabbi on the rampage who exacted religious justice upon the believing community of Jews. Fearing for their lives, many of the Jewish believers fled the area and were scattered throughout the diaspora.

Acts 11:19 ESV   Now those who were scattered because of the persecution that arose over Stephen traveled as far as Phoenicia and Cyprus and Antioch, speaking the word to no one except Jews.

No wonder Ya'akov was pronouncing shalom upon these Jewish believers! These believers were being persecuted by their own religious leaders and kinsmen, like pagans being run out of the land.
Not only does our text affirm the continued existence of the twelve Jewish tribes at this point, but there are many other proofs that they

were still firmly identified by the Jewish community. Even as early as when Cyrus gave his decree in the fifth-century BCE, Jews were seen scattered among the nations.

> **Esther 3:8 ESV** Then Haman said to King Ahasuerus, "There is a certain people scattered abroad and dispersed among the peoples in all the provinces of your kingdom. Their laws are different from those of every other people, and they do not keep the king's laws, so that it is not to the king's profit to tolerate them."

The Jews had maintained the keeping of their own laws, and were seen as being distinct among the nations. In fact, during the first century, at the feast of Shavuot (Pentecost) the diaspora Jews were still clearly being designated.

> **Acts 2:5 ESV** Now there were dwelling in Jerusalem Jews, devout men from every nation under heaven.

> **Acts 2:9-10 ESV** Parthians and Medes and Elamites and residents of Mesopotamia, Judea and Cappadocia, Pontus and Asia, (10) Phrygia and Pamphylia, Egypt and the parts of Libya belonging to Cyrene, and visitors from Rome...

Speaking on this topic, Adam Clarke notes:

> Josephus, Ant. i. 14, cap. 12, tells us that one region could not contain the Jews, but they dwelt in most of the flourishing cities of Asia and Europe, in the islands and continent, not much less in number than the heathen inhabitants. From all this it is evident that the Jews of the dispersion were more numerous than even the Jews in Judea, and that James very properly inscribed this letter to the twelve tribes which were in the dispersion, seeing the twelve tribes really existed then, and do still exist, although not distinguished by separate habitations, as

they were anciently in their own land.[27]

So, the twelve tribes were still counted during this time period, although many were spread throughout the diaspora. However, the view of those Jews living outside of Israel was anything but flattering. We see a glimpse of this in the writings of the Talmud.

> Our Rabbis taught: The generation of the wilderness hath no portion in the world to come, as it is written, 'in this wilderness they shall be consumed, and there they shall die.' 'they shall be consumed,' refers to this world; 'and there they shall die' — to the world to come.[28]

The prayer of Nehemiah as recorded in 2 Maccabees goes like this:

> **2 Maccabees 1:27-29 NJB** Bring together those of us who are dispersed, set free those in slavery among the heathen, look favourably on those held in contempt or abhorrence, and let the heathen know that you are our God. (28) Punish those who oppress us and affront us by their insolence, (29) and plant your people firmly in your Holy Place, as Moses promised.

Advice continues to the Jews who have been scattered:

> **James 1:2-4 MGI** You should have all joy, my brothers, when you enter into various and numerous trials, (3) for you know that the experience of faith causes you to obtain patience. (4) Now patience should have a full work that you may be mature and complete and not lacking in anything.

This advice reflects the rabbinical wisdom of the day. The following is recorded in the Babylonian Talmud:

---

27 Adam Clarke's Commentary on the Bible, The book of James 1:1
28 Babylonian Talmud Mas. Sanhedrin 110b (Soncino Translation)

R. Joshua B. Levi said: He who joyfully bears the chastisements that befall him brings salvation to the world as it is said, "Upon them have we stayed of old, that we might be saved,"[29]

In chapter two of the ancient work entitled "Wisdom of Sirach," which was written in the second century BCE, we read this advice:

> **Sirach 2:1-7 NAB-A**   My son, when you come to serve the LORD, prepare yourself for trials. (2) Be sincere of heart and steadfast, undisturbed in time of adversity. (3) Cling to him, forsake him not; thus will your future be great. (4) Accept whatever befalls you, in crushing misfortune be patient; (5) For in fire gold is tested, and worthy men in the crucible of humiliation. (6) Trust God and he will help you; make straight your ways and hope in him. (7) You who fear the LORD, wait for his mercy, turn not away lest you fall.[30]

The apocryphal work called "The Wisdom of Solomon," which was written some two hundred years before the birth of the Messiah, notes:

> **Wisdom 3:4-6 NAB-A**   For if before men, indeed, they be punished, yet is their hope full of immortality; (5) Chastised a little, they shall be greatly blessed, because God tried them and found them worthy of himself. (6) As gold in the furnace, he proved them, and as sacrificial offerings he took them to himself.

Yes, the Jewish people knew all too well that, at times, they had been chastened for the sake of their overall well-being. And here, in the first century, a wise old sage named Ya'akov reminds them yet again of the chastening which brings about spiritual maturity. The Aramaic term for being "tried, proved or tempted"[31] is pronounced "l'nesyunoa," and is found in what we know as The Lord's Prayer:

---

29 Ibid., Mas Ta'anith 8a (Soncino Translation)
30 The New American Bible w/ Apocrypha Copyright © 1987 by Confraternity of Christian Doctrine, Inc., Washington, DC.
31 Jennings' Lexicon to the Syriac New Testament, pg. 141

Matthew 6:13 ESV   And lead us not into *temptation*, but deliver us from evil.

We find the same word used once again, at the Garden of Gethsemane:

Matthew 26:41 ESV   Watch and pray that you may not enter into *temptation*. The spirit indeed is willing, but the flesh is weak.

1 Corinthians 10:13 ESV   No *temptation* has overtaken you that is not common to man. God is faithful, and he will not let you be tempted beyond your ability, but with the temptation he will also provide the way of escape, that you may be able to endure it.

This lesson, of course, is not only for the person of Jewish decent, but is for all those who would seek to follow the higher road of faith. The writer of the letter to the Hebrews writes:

Hebrews 11:36-40 ESV   Others suffered mocking and flogging, and even chains and imprisonment. (37) They were stoned, they were sawn in two, they were killed with the sword. They went about in skins of sheep and goats, destitute, afflicted, mistreated – (38) of whom the world was not worthy – wandering about in deserts and mountains, and in dens and caves of the earth. (39) And all these, though commended through their faith, did not receive what was promised, (40) since God had provided something better for us, that apart from us they should not be made perfect.

We, too, are a part of a much bigger cosmic plan to bring willing humans into an intimate relationship with their Creator. And seeing that this Creator is a morally perfect Being, those who desire a connection with Him must also enter the path that leads to a more perfect lifestyle.

Matthew 5:11-12 ESV   Blessed are you when others revile you and persecute you and utter all kinds of evil against you falsely on my account. (12) Rejoice and be glad, for your reward is great in heaven, for so they persecuted the prophets who were before you.

This is the gist of it: we're challenged to rise above the profane, and answer the sacred call with those who embrace the Infinite. This call has been heard by men and women throughout the ages, cloistered in abbeys and hermitages, who considered the putting off of the flesh and the forsaking of life's frivolities but a small price for the mystical[32] relationship with God.

But, our wise sage reminds us that this kind of relationship doesn't come easily! This type of relationship isn't obtained through the act of acquiring information, but rather comes through practice, through disciplined living, and through trusting God!

The Aramaic word for "entering into" this circumstance of being tempted is shown using an imperfect verb , ܐܠܘܬ (t'eluw), which describes the situation for moral growth as one which is on-going. It's not a one-time experience, but a process through which the person "enters" at one level, then after a time exits at another. As one author describes, It's this "discipline that leads to improvement."[33] Those of us in the western world prefer one-time events, one-step processes by which decisions are made, opinions are adjusted, and character flaws are fixed. But life is seldom like that. Usually, humans require a consistent process for real change to occur and, according to Ya'akov, for maturity to take place. And, these are the very building blocks upon which a disciple is born. For every Rabbi knew the opening words of Mishna Avoth:

---

32 The use of the term "mystical" here is meant as a general designation for the relationship between the human and the divine.

33 Plumptre, The Cambridge Bible for Schools and Colleges, Commentary on James ch. 1:4

Mishnah 1 Moses received the Torah at Sinai and transmitted it to Joshua, Joshua to the elders, and the elders to the prophets, and the prophets to the men of the great synagogue. The latter used to say three things: Be patient in [the administration of] justice, rear many disciples and make a fence round the Torah.[34]

Similarly, these three elements can also be discerned among the departing words of the Messiah on the Mount of Olives:

Matthew 28:18-20 ESV And Jesus came and said to them, "All authority in heaven and on earth has been given to me. (19) Go therefore and make disciples of all nations, baptizing them in the name of the Father and of the Son and of the Holy Spirit, (20) teaching them to observe all that I have commanded you. And behold, I am with you always, to the end of the age."

Now, back to Ya'akov's letter:

James 1:5 MGI Now if any of you lacks wisdom, he should ask [for it] from God, who gives generously to all and does not reproach, and it will be given to him.

There's an ancient Greek maxim which says:

Αρχη γνωσεως της αγνοιας ή γνωσις.

"The knowledge of ignorance is the beginning of knowledge."[35]

In the fifth verse, Ya'akov describes a person who recognizes that he lacks wisdom. This is also the crux of the problem, because the foolish person can't imagine that he isn't wise, whereas the wise person is the one who is fully aware that he is indeed foolish!

---

34 Mishna – Mas. Avoth 1:1 (Soncino Translation)
35 As quoted by Adam Clarke in his commentary on James 1:5

Solomon wrote:

> **Proverbs 2:3-6 ESV**   ...yes, if you call out for insight and raise your voice for understanding, (4) if you seek it like silver and search for it as for hidden treasures, (5) then you will understand the fear of the LORD and find the knowledge of God. (6) For the LORD gives wisdom; from his mouth come knowledge and understanding;...

This "asking," that Ya'akov is talking about marks a trait found in the follower of God.   It's an imperfect verb in the Peshitta text which suggests a lifestyle and pattern for approaching God. It describes a steady flow of requests being made by the follower to God, which begins with the self-awareness and recognition that the follower is "lacking, deficient, or wanting."[36] This person regularly finds himself in need of God's counsel.

In the structure of this sentence, the focus is upon the need to ask regularly and consistently. The promise, of course, is spectacular! "It will be given him."

Solomon had a lot to say about humanity's need for wisdom. Here's an example in chapter two:

> **Proverbs 2:1-10 ESV**   My son, if you receive my words and treasure up my commandments with you, (2) making your ear attentive to wisdom and inclining your heart to understanding; (3) yes, if you call out for insight and raise your voice for understanding, (4) if you seek it like silver and search for it as for hidden treasures, (5) then you will understand the fear of the LORD and find the knowledge of God. (6) For the LORD gives wisdom; from his mouth come knowledge and understanding; (7) he stores up sound wisdom for the upright; he is a shield to those who walk in integrity, (8) guarding the paths of justice and

---

36 ܚܣܝܪ "chasiyr," Payne Smith's Compendious Syriac Dictionary, pg. 151

watching over the way of his saints. (9) Then you will understand righteousness and justice and equity, every good path; (10) for wisdom will come into your heart, and knowledge will be pleasant to your soul...

Don't miss the connection that Solomon makes between the person who receives wisdom and the person who practices God's words. We find this same ongoing theme in Ya'akov's letter. Ya'akov says that the person who is serious about approaching God is the person who demonstrates his seriousness through his actions, and his lifestyle.

So, now for the million dollar question: What is wisdom?

The primary term for wisdom is חָכְמָה "chokmah" in Hebrew, and "Khekmat" in Aramaic. Properly "chokmah" means: *"to be wise, clever, cunning, shrewd."*[37]

Harris defines it like this:

> The essential idea of hakam (*it's noun form*) represents a manner of thinking and attitude concerning life's experiences; including matters of general interest and basic morality. These concerns relate to prudence in secular affairs, skills in the arts, moral sensitivity, and experience in the ways of the Lord.[38]

True wisdom, according to the Bible, is directly linked to how a person perceives, thinks, and responds to life experiences based upon their personal knowledge of, and relationship to, God. In fact, the Messiah Himself is seen as being the personification of true Wisdom.

In Proverbs, we read:

Proverbs 3:19 ESV The LORD by wisdom founded the earth; by understanding he established the heavens;

---

37 See Brown, Driver, Briggs' Hebrew Lexicon, entry " חָכַם "
38 TWOT article "hakam, hokma" pg. 282

And this is written in the book of Jeremiah:

> **Jeremiah 10:12 ESV** It is he who made the earth by his power, who established the world by his wisdom, and by his understanding stretched out the heavens.

In each example, it's the Creator's "chokmah" which created the world. And yet, in the letter to the Hebrews and the good news according to Yochanon we read this concerning the Messiah:

> **Hebrews 1:2 ESV** ...but in these last days He has spoken to us by His Son, whom He appointed the heir of all things, through whom also He created the world.

> **John 1:1-3 ESV** In the beginning was the Word, and the Word was with God, and the Word was God. (2) He was in the beginning with God. (3) All things were made through Him, and without Him was not any thing made that was made.

The Messiah is Chokmah! Look at these New Testament passages.

> **John 2:24 ESV** But Jesus on his part did not entrust himself to them, because *he knew all people.*

> **John 16:30 ESV** Now we know that *you know all things* and do not need anyone to question you; this is why we believe that you came from God.

> **John 21:17 ESV** He said to him the third time, "Simon, son of John, do you love me?" Peter was grieved because he said to him the third time, "Do you love me?" and he said to him, "Lord, *you know everything*; you know that I love you." Jesus said to him, "Feed my sheep."

In chapter three, Ya'akov tells us the original source of this chokmah. He says:

James 3:17 Murdock   But *the wisdom which is from above*, is pure, and full of peace, and mild, and submissive, and full of compassion and of good fruits, and without partiality, and without respect of persons.

Wisdom, the Chokmah of God; the Messiah who came from above, and who, through the promise of the Ruach (Spirit), offers His wisdom now to us.

Rabbi Sha'ul boldly proclaims:

1 Corinthians 2:16 Murdock   For who has known the mind of the Lord, that he should instruct him? But we have the mind of the Messiah.

Ya'akov adds this statement that gives us hope:

James 1:5 Murdock   And if any of you lacks wisdom, let him ask [it] of God, who gives to all freely, and reproaches not; and it will be given him.

Chapter 3

During 2010, I visited an Egyptian Temple known as "The Temple of Man." Its proper name is the Temple of Luxor. As I looked around the temple, I was confronted everywhere by large human statues of men, carved as in motion. In fact, the whole temple seems to be laid out as a human body busy in some type of action. Well, this is a perfect image for us as we begin the next leg of our journey in the book of Ya'akov.

Ya'akov will now bring a subject into focus that he will keep as one of the central points until the end of the letter. And that point is faith.

Biblical faith has frequently been misunderstood, due in part to a disconnect between the original culture and the term itself. It is also misinterpreted by an ever-evolving religious theological community. Since we each lead our own life and have our own faith, it also becomes a personal issue.

Let's start by examining the passage Ya'akov uses to develop this religious concept.

Let's begin in verse three where the term is first introduced.

> **James 1:3,4-5 MGI** ...for you know that the experience of faith causes you to obtain patience... (5) Now if any of you lacks wisdom, he should ask [for it] from God, who gives generously to all and does not reproach and it will be given to him. (6) But he should ask in faith, not doubting, for he who doubts is like the waves of the sea that the wind stirs up.

Before we look at why we need faith, let's make sure that we understand what Ya'akov means by the term.

The Aramaic word here is: b'haymanuwt ,a)[39] = (ܒܗܲܝܡܵܢܘܼܬ݂)
which comes from the rootword: hamen = (ܗܲܡܸܢ)

This probably reminds us of our English word "amen" and indeed it should, for this is where our word finds it's origin. This word is typically translated into English simply as "faith."

It's sister term in Hebrew is "emunah." Again, this is almost always translated into English simply as "faith." But, what is biblical faith?

Properly, emunah means: *"faithfulness; truth, stability, steady, truly."*[40] It's closer root word "aman" means: *"to be firm, secure, dependable."*[41]

But, where does this extremely ancient word itself come from? The answer: *water.* Faith originally finds it's origin from man's observation of the connection between water and life.

Here's how the concept of "faith" was originally formed. It started off with the first letter in the Hebrew alphabet, the aleph. This letter was originally designated by a picture of an ox. It indicates a strong one, one who assists man with its strength. Early on, this letter became associated with God – the One who is strong. In fact, it could be out of this designation for God that the symbol and likeness to a strong ox is actually fixed. In fact, our earliest designation for God is found in the Hebrew letters aleph and the lamed, it forms the Hebrew word "El" which can be seen in terms such as: Elohim or El Shaddai. The designation "El" in it's ancient picture form indicates one who is a "strong shepherd." That indicates that God is like a Strong Shepherd, guiding and caring for mankind. Now, back to our explanation of man's concept for "faith."

Each of the primary terms for faith come from three Hebrew letters:

---

39 SEDRA3 transliterated designation.
40 Benner, Ancient Hebrew Lexicon of the Bible, "emunah" pg. 171
41 Jenni & Westermann, Theological Lexicon of the Old Testament, "aman" pg. 134

The aleph, the mem, and the nun. We know what the aleph stood for in the ancient world. It was the picture of a "strong one." Likewise, the ancient way of drawing the Hebrew letter mem was with a symbol for "water." Even today, "mayim" is the Hebrew word for "water."

So, let's put these two symbols together which then can express compound concepts, ideas, and ultimately, "faith." First we have the symbol for strength, and added to that we have the symbol for water. Simply put this means: "*strong water.*"

Now, let's add our final letter, the "nun." The Hebrew letter nun was used as the designation for life. Sometimes it was drawn like fish swimming – indicating life, or even as a seed which would later sprout. This was a symbol for life, as well. Together, these three letters form the Hebrew term "Amen," which probably had as its original intended meaning: "*strong water brings forth life.*"

This makes sense to me because our first two letters, the aleph and the mem, make the Hebrew word, "em," which means: "*mother.*" You see it's the mother which brings forth life through powerfully strong water. The water breaks and the pregnant mother brings forth life. We can't breathe in water after we're born, yet we exist in this water while we're still forming. It's strong water! It's powerful water! It's magical water! That makes sense.

All kinds of concepts come from this ancient imagery of the mother, strong water, and life. This same Hebrew designation for mother, "em," when it's pronounced "am" means both "*glue*" and "*arm.*"[42] This makes sense, since it's the mother who holds the child securely in her arms. And it's the mother who is seen as holding the family together[43]. A cubit was a source of measurement the same length as the arm. The cubit was the standard length of measurement in the ancient world, as were the mother's arms the standard length of a child's security.

This powerful picture from the past helps us to see why it might be that

42 Benner notes that "am" is where the English term "arm" is derived.
43 See AHLB, pg. 55ff

this particular word was used to describe our relationship with God. It creates a picture of us being held in the arms of ultimate security and safety. It is imagery of well-being and nourishment. And it's from this nourishment that another generation goes forth and carries the bloodline and the family's name. It's important to see that action comes out of being embraced.

There is one more thing we need to grasp before we can fully understand Ya'akov's usage of this Hebrew term for faith. We must understand it's contrast to the Greek term used to translate this idea. It's the Greek way of thinking that comes with the translation, which has almost completely defined the modern-day Christian faith.

Let's turn our eyes briefly to the Greek New Testament. The word "pistis" is the primary Greek term used here to translate both terms "amen" and "emunah" and their Aramaic equivalents.

The typical Greek definition of "pistis" can be seen in the following Strong's Concordance designation:

G4102 πίστις pistis *pis'-tis*

From G3982; *persuasion*, that is, *credence*; moral *conviction* (of *religious* truth, or the truthfulness of God or a religious teacher), especially *reliance* upon Christ for salvation; abstractly *constancy* in such profession; by extension the system of religious (Gospel) *truth* itself: - assurance, belief, believe, faith, fidelity.

In classical Greek, pistis is used extensively for one's *perspective* of an individual towards a given word, contract, oath or to complete an act. More accurately, it denotes one's *perspective* regarding how another will keep their word, a contract, an oath, or an act. However, this word is not about the act itself. Pistis is a term of thinking, not one of doing.

This is absolutely not what the biblical authors were communicating, because this is not biblical thinking. The bible is not focused on thought, rather, it is focused upon action.

The author of the Letter to the Hebrews chose to use this exact Aramaic word for faith – the same word found in our text of James – when he writes about the heroes. Let's take a look at what they share in common.

> **Hebrews 11:4 ESV** By faith **Abel** *offered* to God a more acceptable sacrifice than Cain...

> **Hebrews 11:5 ESV** By faith **Enoch** was taken up so that he should not see death, and he was not found, because God had taken him. Now before he was taken he was commended as having pleased God.

Do we know what Enoch did to be found pleasing to God?

> **Jude 1:14 ESV** It was also about these that Enoch, the seventh from Adam, *prophesied*, saying, "Behold, the Lord comes with ten thousands of his holy ones...

Jewish tradition holds that Enoch was an obedient prophet of God. It's also interesting that Enoch lived a certain amount of time.

> **Genesis 5:23 ESV** Thus all the days of Enoch were 365 years.

Ancient tradition holds that Enoch was not only a prophet, but a prophet who could tell the times and the seasons by the stars. And, ironically he lived to the number which would become the universally accepted number designating a year. He was a prophet who was connected with the telling of times and seasons indeed! The bottom line here is that Enoch acted upon what he knew to be the message of God.

> **Hebrews 11:7 ESV** By faith **Noah**, being warned by God concerning events as yet unseen, in reverent fear *constructed an ark* for the saving of his household.

Hebrews 11:8 ESV By faith **Abraham** obeyed when he was called to go out to a place that he was to receive as an inheritance. And *he went out*, not knowing where he was going.

(In all of these examples of faith, we find that each person acted upon what God had shown or told them.)

Hebrews 11:11 ESV By faith **Sarah** herself *received power* to conceive, even when she was past the age, since she considered him faithful who had promised.

This is probably not the best way to render the Aramaic verb "nesb'et." The Syriac Dictionary uses this same word in the following sentences: *"To take a wife," "he adopted a son," "to take a memorial," "to gain a victory," "to take for an example," "to take account," "to take counsel."*[44]

In each of these is an example of action. Sarah took action, and God gave her the ability to conceive a child. Sarah not only "considered" God faithful, but she put her feet into action and lived out that faith by her daily obedience to God. (Just read her story in the pages of the book of Genesis.)

Hebrews 11:17 ESV By faith **Abraham**, when he was tested, *offered up Isaac...*

Hebrews 11:20 ESV By faith **Isaac** *invoked future blessings* on Jacob and Esau.

(This, of course, is only one example among many which I could have listed from the life of Yitzak.)

Hebrews 11:21 ESV By faith **Jacob**, when dying, *blessed* each of the sons of Joseph, bowing in worship over the head of his staff.

---

44 See Payne Smith's A Compendious Syriac Dictionary, pg. 341

Hebrews 11:22 ESV   By faith **Joseph**, at the end of his life, *made mention* of the exodus of the Israelites and *gave directions* concerning his bones.

Hebrews 11:28 ESV   By faith he (*Moses*) *kept the Passover and sprinkled the blood,* so that the Destroyer of the firstborn might not touch them.

Hebrews 11:29 ESV   By faith **the people** *crossed the Red Sea* as on dry land...

Hebrews 11:31 ESV   By faith **Rahab** the prostitute did not perish with those who were disobedient, because she *had given a friendly welcome* to the spies.

Of course, Rahab did much more than just that. She risked her own life because of her faith in this God of the Hebrews.

Hebrews 11:32 ESV   And what more shall I say? For time would fail me to tell of **Gideon, Barak, Samson, Jephthah**, of **David** and **Samuel** and **the prophets**-- (33) who through faith *conquered kingdoms, enforced justice, obtained promises, stopped the mouths of lions,* (34) *quenched the power of fire, escaped the edge of the sword, were made strong out of weakness, became mighty in war, put foreign armies to flight...*

Action! Each person put their relationship with God into motion, and did something about what they knew. You cannot separate personal action from biblical faith or you are left with nothing more than a mere philosophy!

Jeff Benner (an expert on the ancient Hebrew culture), puts it this way:

When the Hebrew word emunah is translated as faith,

misconceptions of its meaning occur. Faith is usually perceived as a knowing, while the Hebrew emunah is a firm action. To have faith in God is not knowing that God exists or knowing that he will act, rather it is that the one with emunah will act with firmness toward God's will.[45]

Life comes from the oceans. The first woman brings forth life out of breaking water. Mankind is offered new life through the strong waters of the flood. It's with the washing of water that the priests are deemed consecrated. It's through the waters of baptism that the promise of a new life springs forth. Water! Man discovered right away that he couldn't live without it. And maybe this symbol is what John is referring to when he speaks of being "born through water and blood," in 1 John 5:6.

Biblical faith stands contrary to the philosophies of the ancient world. It stands on the evidence that "actions speak louder than words." From this we know that actual biblical faith may better be defined as: *"action because of the One who holds us."*

If you really believe something, you'll act upon it and do something about it. If you don't act, you don't really believe.

That's the message we just saw in the eleventh chapter of Hebrews. But, don't miss the fact that in none of those examples did we see blind faith. Each person followed what God had instructed him or her to do. It would be a huge mistake to think that biblical faith means a person does whatever he/she "feels inspired" to do. That is an inaccurate (yet very popular) modern idea about faith. Real, authentic, biblical faith begins when we follow the revealed instructions of God.

Ya'akov didn't study under Plato, Aristotle, or any other Greek philosopher. Ya'akov was a Jew's Jew who was thought to have studied under the school of Hillel. And he tells us to act! As a matter of fact, if

---

45 AHLB # 1290-C (d1)

we put feet to our faith, then we're thinking biblically!

> **James 1:6 MGI** But he should ask in faith, not doubting, for he who doubts is like the waves of the sea that the wind stirs up.

Because we know this One who holds us, we take action as a loving response – consistently, and without wavering.

This analogy reminds me of another situation where "emunah" is used. This particular example might help us to better understand what Ya'akov is trying to express.

> **Exodus 17:8-13 ESV** Then Amalek came and fought with Israel at Rephidim. (9) So Moses said to Joshua, "Choose for us men, and go out and fight with Amalek. Tomorrow I will stand on the top of the hill with the staff of God in my hand." (10) So Joshua did as Moses told him, and fought with Amalek, while Moses, Aaron, and Hur went up to the top of the hill. (11) Whenever Moses held up his hand, Israel prevailed, and whenever he lowered his hand, Amalek prevailed. (12) But Moses' hands grew weary, so they took a stone and put it under him, and he sat on it, while Aaron and Hur held up his hands, one on one side, and the other on the other side. So his hands were steady until the going down of the sun. (13) And Joshua overwhelmed Amalek and his people with the sword.

The word that the Jews used for faith is right here in our text. It's the word that describes the position of Moses' hand which caused the battle to be won: Steady! Yes, the Hebrew word for "steady" is "emunah." In the example of the battle at Rephidim and Moses' hand, we see that when His hand was "steady," Joshua was winning the battle. By the same token, when Moses' hand was "unsteady," fluctuating up and down, Joshua began losing the battle.

Faith in God is not only that which acts because of the relationship.

Biblical faith is that which succeeds when it's steady.

In the Talmud, the rabbis state that the disappearance of "men of faith" will bring about the downfall of the world.[46] This is a subject we should take very seriously.

Yeshua (Jesus) said of this same type of faith:

> **Matthew 21:21-22 ESV**   And Jesus answered them, "Truly, I say to you, if you have faith and do not doubt, you will not only do what has been done to the fig tree, but even *if you say* to this mountain, 'Be taken up and thrown into the sea,' it will happen. (22) And whatever you ask in prayer, you will receive, if you have faith."

The Aramaic verb for "if you say" describe a consistent faith that is not in a constant state of wavering. That's exactly what Ya'akov is conveying: don't waver, don't doubt, or like waves on the sea you'll be tossed about.

The Jewish commentary on Psalm 119:46 describes those whose faith waivers as those "who grasp the rope by both ends," or like those who waver between God and Baal.[47] The idea is that when you grasp a rope at both ends it becomes ineffective, useless.

Another way of describing Ya'akov's word for "doubting" is "*to have a divided mind.*" This is the same word used for the Roman guards as they were "dividing" the Master's robe at the crucifixion.

It can also be translated: "*to hesitate.*" When you have two conflicting thoughts, you hesitate in your actions. Remembering that Ya'akov's letter is to the twelve Jewish tribes, this text speaks of having divided loyalties.

David wrote:

---

46 Babylonian Talmud, Sotah 9.12
47 Midrash on Psalm 119:46 as quoted in The Jewish Annotated New Testament, pg 428

Psalms 119:113 ESV Samekh. I hate the double-minded, but I love your law (*Torah*).

And in the book of Enoch we find this:

Enoch 41.4 "Draw not nigh to uprightness with a double heart, and associate not with those of a double heart".

By the way, the word used for the phrase "asking in faith" from verse six is an imperfect verb in the Aramaic language. This means that we should always be in a constant lifestyle of asking God, and not hesitate in our actions.

> **James 1:7-8 MGI** And that man should not expect to receive anything from the LORD, (8) who doubts in his mind and is troubled in all his ways.

Rabbi Tanchum, commenting on Deuteronomy 26:17 said:

"Behold, the Scripture exhorts the Israelites, and tells them when they pray that they should not have two hearts, one for the holy blessed God, and one for something else."[48]

So, we leave this chapter with a fresh call to be focused in our devotions, serious about our convictions, and immediate in our actions.

---

48 As quoted by Adam Clarke in his commentary on James chapter 1

Chapter 4

In the last chapter we explored the biblical concept of faith. Our fresh understanding of this concept should reshape our understanding of such passages as this well-known verse:

> **John 3:16 Murdock** For God so loved the world, that he gave his only begotten Son, that whosoever believes on him, should not perish, but should have life eternal.

> "believe" = (Heb) Emunah = active believing
> *i.e. action, behavior, following.*

If the true message of faith had been presented over the years, followers of the Messiah may have been pressed to a much higher level of service, sacrifice, and change.

> **James 1:9-11 MGI**   And the humble brother should boast in his lifted position (10) and the rich in his humility, because as the flower of an herb, likewise he passes away. (11) For the sun will rise with its heat and will dry up the herb and its flower will fall and the beauty of its appearance will be destroyed. So also the rich [man] withers in his ways.

The context of this section is a continuation of the discussion on life's trials. Ya'akov says:

1. Calculate them as a means of joy. (v.2)
2. Be mindful that their purpose is to develop patience. (v.3)
3. They drive you to becoming complete. (v.4)

4. The end result is that you'll lack nothing. (v.4)
5. Ask God for wisdom to understand and endure. (v.5)

Don't waiver during the trial, but trust God. (v.6-8)

Did you notice that the goal of trials is to make the follower of the Messiah "complete?"

> **v.4** Now patience should have a full work that you may be mature and complete and not lacking in anything.

The Aramaic word used here for "perfect" or "complete" is meshamleya It comes from the Root: Shaphel. It means: *"full; complete; perfect; filled."*[49]

Here are a couple more scriptures that use this word and show it's intended meaning as used in James.

> **1 John 1:4 ESV** And we are writing these things so that our joy may be *complete*.

> **1 John 4:18 ESV** There is no fear in love, but *perfect* love casts out fear. For fear has to do with punishment, and whoever fears has not been *perfected* in love.

It's Hebrew sister word is "Shalam:" *"to be at peace, to be complete, to be finished, to be ended."*[50] This term, "shalam" is found throughout the writings of the TaNaK to indicate: *a "perfect" heart.*

Here's an example found in first Kings:

> **1 Kings 8:61 LBP** Let your heart therefore be *perfect* with the LORD our God, to walk in his ways and to keep his

---

49 See SEDRA3 entry "MaShamlyoa"
50 Brown, Driver and Briggs' Hebrew Lexicon #7999 "Shalam"

commandments, his covenant, his judgments, and his laws, as at this day.[51]

"Shalam" can also be used to indicate being *whole* or *completed* as in the stones used for the altar.

> **Deuteronomy 27:6 NET**   You must build the altar of the LORD your God with *whole* stones and offer burnt offerings on it to the LORD your God.[52]

This word is also used of the dressed stones for the temple which the tools of man had neither touched nor formed.

> **1 Kings 6:7 ESV**   When the house was built, it was with stone *prepared* at the quarry, so that neither hammer nor axe nor any tool of iron was heard in the house while it was being built.

This imagery certainly speaks of the future, where the believers are being built together with one another into a house of worship for God. And the shaping isn't done with human tools, but by the hand of God alone. Look at the following passages that speak to this same topic:

> **Ephesians 2:22 ESV**   In him you also *are being built* together into a dwelling place for God *by the Spirit.*

> **Colossians 2:6-7 ESV**   Therefore, *as you received* Christ Jesus the Lord, so walk in him, (7) rooted and *built up* in him and established in the faith, just as you were taught, abounding in thanksgiving.

Now, concerning "shalam's" related term, "shalom" (although these are basically the same word), Laird Harris says:

---

51 Holy Bible From The Ancient Eastern Texts: Aramaic Of The Peshitta by George M. Lamsa (1933)
52 NET Bible® copyright © 1996-2006 by Biblical Studies Press, L.L.C. www.bible.org. All rights reserved.

Shalom is the result of God's activity in covenant (berit), and is the result of righteousness (Isa_32:17). In nearly two-thirds of its occurrences, shalom describes the state of *fulfillment* which is the result of God's presence... "The general meaning behind the root sh-l-m is of completion and fulfillment-of entering into a state of wholeness and unity, a restored relationship."[53]

That is exactly the completeness that Ya'akov is discussing. He says that the bearing up under trials and pressures brings us to a closer state of spiritual completeness, fulfillment and intimacy with God. That's the goal of this whole thing.

Let me further quote from Harris' article, which says:

"Shelem is also identified... as a 'communion sacrifice,' i.e. one in which there is a sharing of the sacrificial animal and the resultant fellowship around a meal... the fact that the shelem usually comes last in the lists of the offerings... has prompted some scholars to argue that this is a "concluding sacrifice." This derives shelem from the rare Piel meaning "to complete." If this sense is correct, the NT references to Christ our Peace. Eph 2:14) become more meaningful, as he is the final sacrifice for us Heb_9:27; Heb_9:10:Heb_9:12) . Hebrews 9:9,11 ESV   ... (which is symbolic for the present age). According to this arrangement, gifts and sacrifices are offered that cannot *perfect* the conscience of the worshiper...

(11) But when Christ appeared as a high priest of the good things that have come, then through the greater and more *perfect* tent (not made with hands, that is, not of this creation)[54]

Remember that Ya'akov's audience is made up of Jews. They would totally understand these Hebrew and Aramaic terms. Ya'akov is

---

53 Theological Wordbook of the Old Testament, R. Laird Harris, Gleason L. Archer, Jr. & Bruse K. Waltke. copyright © 1980 Moody Press, All rights reserved. Entry #2401 "shalem".
54 TWOT 2401 "shelem".

saying: *"let trials make you this..."*

Now, usually you can learn something about a word by understanding how it's translated into another language. When the translators translated this word for "complete" or "perfect" in Ya'akov's letter they used the Greek term "teleios" which Strongs' describes as: *"complete (in various applications of labor, growth, mental and moral character, etc.); neuter (as noun, with G3588) completeness: - of full age, man, perfect."*[55]

Now, let's tie together what we now know of the Hebrew/Aramaic with the Greek. Here, I believe we can gain insights from Adam Clarke's comments on the translated word "teleios," as used in Ya'akov's letter. (This is brilliant.) He writes:

> A victim was ΤΕλΕιΟς, perfect, that was perfectly sound, having no disease; it was ὁλοκληρος, entire, if it had all its members, having nothing redundant, nothing deficient. Be then to the Lord what he required his sacrifices to be; let your whole heart, your body, soul, and spirit, be sanctified to the Lord of hosts, that he may fill you with all his fullness.[56]

The intent then of these trials is to cause us to become more like our Master, who was entirely complete, entirely whole. And because of His completeness and wholeness, He was the perfect sacrifice. We also become perfect, living sacrifices through the pressure of these trials in order to be conformed to His image. This, then, is the required maturing element we need to make us complete. Like steel is refined to make it strong, so we are refined by trials to make us complete. And that will make us fitting for the One who calls us to be His bride.

In fact, it's this concept in Ya'akov that is an echo of the Master's own words in the teaching of the Sermon on the Mount.

---

55 Strong's Hebrew and Greek Dictionaries of Hebrew and Greek Words taken from Strong's Exhaustive Concordance by James Strong, S.T.D., LL.D., 1890.

56 Adam Clarke's Commentary on the Bible, Adam Clarke, LL.D., F.S.A., (1715-1832) notes on James 1:4

Matthew 5:48 ESV   You therefore must be *perfect* (teleioi), as your heavenly Father is *perfect* (teleios).

Ya'akov's letter is filled with references to his half-brothers'[57] sermons and teaching. *(In just eleven verses of chapter one Ya'akov has made reference to Yeshua's teachings in the Sermon on the Mount four times!)*

James 1:2 Murdock   Let it be all joy to you, my brethren, when ye enter into many and various trials.

Compare that to the Sermon on the Mount:

Matthew 5:11 Murdock   Blessed are ye, when they revile you and persecute you, and speak every evil thing against you, falsely, on my account.

James 1:4 Murdock   And let patience have its perfect work, so that ye may be complete and perfect, and may lack nothing.

Matthew 5:48 Murdock   Be ye therefore perfect; even as your Father who is in heaven is perfect.

In James 1:5 he writes on the subject of asking:

James 1:5 Murdock   And if any of you lacks wisdom, let him ask [it] of God, who giveth to all freely, and reproaches not; and it will be given him.

In the Sermon on the Mount we see Yeshua has already instructed on the very same topic:

Matthew 7:7 Murdock   Ask, and it shall be given to you: seek, and ye shall find: knock, and it shall be opened to you.

---

57 I use this designation loosely when referring to Ya'akov's familial relationship to the Messiah.

Next:

> **James 1:9 Murdock** And let the depressed brother rejoice, in his elevation;

In the Sermon on the Mount, we find the very same topic and contrast:

> **Matthew 5:3 Murdock** Blessed are the poor in spirit for the kingdom of heaven is theirs!

There are more references to Yeshua's teaching in the Sermon on the Mount throughout Ya'akov's letter than anywhere else in scripture. I'll continue to point them out as Ya'akov teaches from them in his text.

> **James 1:9 MGI** And the humble brother should boast in his lifted position...

Notice that it's the depressed or lowly man that is called "brother." He is the one who is "mak'iykoa" or *humble, lowly, mild and gentle.*[58]

Contrast this brother who is ultimately lifted by the Lord, to the one we see in the next verse:

> **James 1:10 MGI** ...and the rich in his humility, because as the flower of an herb, likewise he passes away.

No mention here of the term "brother" but, the mention of being like a flower who "passes away."

Ya'akov lived as His Master lived – humbly, with little regard for the wealth of the world. It makes me wonder what a godly example Yosef must have been for these young men. Raised in a humble Jewish home, in a small village. We're told that mom and dad were too poor to offer

---

58 SEDRA3, entry "mak'iykoa"

anything more than a poor man's offering.[59] At some point in time early in his adult life, his father passes away and he is forced to take on the responsibility for the care of his brothers and sisters and the young step-mother. Maybe you're thinking that Miryam was working in their little town as well. Actually, it would have been tough for a woman who was considered unfaithful to her betrothed husband to find much work anywhere.[60] The sons of Yosef understood what it meant to live humbly. They were probably extremely poor!

We also see this same lifestyle and teaching of humble living throughout Yeshua's ministry. He was the One who said that He had no place to lay His head.[61] It would be easy to contrast this simple, humble lifestyle with the absurd theologies today of the 'name-it-and-claim-it' and the prosperity doctrines that stand in direct conflict with the clear teaching and examples from the scriptures.

Our writer continues:

> **James 1:11 MGI** For the sun will rise with its heat and will dry up the herb and its flower will fall and the beauty of its appearance will be destroyed. So also the rich [man] withers in his ways.

Here, Ya'akov uses the familiar imagery of the hot sharav wind which blows through the Israeli landscape. It's the same picture of east wind used as imagery by Isaiah:

> **Isaiah 40:6-9 ESV** A voice says, "Cry!" And I said, "What shall I cry?" All flesh is grass, and all its beauty is like the flower of the field. (7) The grass withers, the flower fades when the breath of the LORD blows on it; surely the people are grass. (8) The grass

---

59 See Luke 2:24 where the offering for those who are poor is being described.
60 Even though scripture makes it clear that Miryam had not been unfaithful to Yosef, this was the local gossip.
61 See Luke 9:58.

withers, the flower fades, but the word of our God will stand forever. (9) Go on up to a high mountain, O Zion, herald of good news; lift up your voice with strength, O Jerusalem, herald of good news; lift it up, fear not; say to the cities of Judah, "Behold your God!"

Isaiah concludes this section with the lifting up of that which was low. David does much the same thing to describe the "one who is afflicted and fainting."

> **Psalms 102:4,11 ESV**   My heart is struck down like grass and has withered; I forget to eat my bread... (11) My days are like an evening shadow; I wither away like grass.

Sound familiar? Almost assuredly it's these passages that Ya'akov has in mind when he talks about the two contrasting kinds of people, the humble and the rich, the one who will fade and the other who will be elevated. Both passages conclude with the giving of hope to the downtrodden and the oppressed.

> **Psalms 102:16-17 ESV**   For the LORD builds up Zion; he appears in his glory; (17) he regards the prayer of the destitute and does not despise their prayer.

In the same way that God "builds up Zion" and "hears the prayer of the destitute," God also "builds up" or "elevates" the humble. So, the lowly man is lifted up and the lofty man is made low.

This perfection or completion has to do with the work that only God can do in the life of the believer. In the same way the temple is built, and in the same way that the peace offering brings things to completion, only the hand of God through trials can bring wholeness and completeness in our lives.

And why would Ya'akov, at the very beginning of his letter, be so determined to point out the distinction between the rich and the poor, and the reality of trials for the Jews? It's because the Jews where Ya'akov is living and serving, have been going through the aftermath of a severe famine. Between the years 44 and 45 CE, an intense famine swept through the area of Jerusalem. The Jewish believers had been going through terrible trials! The leader of this Jewish movement wants to make sure that he tells the Jews outside of Jerusalem that he understands and can empathize with their problems, too.

Chapter 5

In the last chapter we discussed Ya'akov's take on the trials of life.

We then took notice of how he contrasted the poor man with the rich, each of whom faced trials, but only one was considered a brother.

The Tanakh has a lot to say about trials. Here's one example:

> **Exodus 20:20 ESV**   Moses said to the people, "Do not fear, for God has come to test you, that the fear of Him may be before you, that you may not sin."

Because of this and other scriptures on the same topic, the rabbis had a lot to say about the source and purpose of trials. In the Midrash Rabbah we read:

> Happy the man who can withstand the test, for there is none whom God does not prove. He tries the rich man to see if his hand will be opened unto the poor, and the poor man He tries in order to see whether he will accept chastisement without repining, as it says, And that thou bring the poor that are humbled to thy house (Isa. LVIII, 7). If the rich man withstand his test and practice charity, then he will enjoy his wealth in this world, while the capital will be preserved for him in the Life to Come, and the Holy One, blessed be He, will, moreover, redeem him from the punishment of Gehinnom, as it says, Happy is he that considers the poor; the Lord will deliver him in the day of evil - (Ps. XLI, 2).[62]

Likewise, Ya'akov also turns his attention to the benefits that trials offer for the life to come.

---

62 Midrash Rabbah, Exodus 31.3 (Soncino edition)

> **James 1:12 MGI** Blessed [is] the man who endures trials, so that when he is examined, he may receive the crown of life that God promised to those who love him.

Ya'akov tells us that if we endure temptation then something really good will happen. But, before we get to the really good thing that will happen, what does he mean by "enduring"?

The word Ya'akov uses here for *endure* is the Aramaic term *d'amsayb'ar.* This term can be translated as *"to preach, to declare, to bear, to endure, to be nourished, to be fed."*[63]

We often think of enduring as just holding it together in the midst of a difficult situation, when really it means far more than just that. The term "enduring temptation," is an active participle used in the Paiel form. That means Ya'akov is referring to an enduring which doesn't stay the same but actually continues to increase. It's used in such phrases as "to make warm, to heat up" and "to give warmth."[64] This term is used by the Master in the book of Matthew:

> **Matthew 24:13**   "But the one who *endures* to the end will be saved."[65]

Here again, this enduring is much more than just hanging in there! More so, it is the ever increasing message one conveys throughout and because of the experience! What do you *preach* during a trial? What does your life say to others when the heat is turned up and the pressure is on? This is the point of Ya'akov's message. And in verse twelve, he goes on to say, once he has done that, he will receive a reward.

---

63 see entry in SEDRA3
64 Thackston, W.M., Introduction to Syriac, pg. 123
65 English Standard Version

> **v.12** Blessed [is] the man who endures trials, so that when he is examined, he may receive the crown of life that God promised to those who love him.

When this person is finally *"proved, examined, and inspected"*[66] he'll receive "a crown of life."

This promise was extremely important in the first few centuries of Christian persecution where those who were baptized were then crowned anticipating martyrdom.[67] They desired to be crowned like their Master was crowned, preceding His martyrdom.[68] Remember the first martyr of the faith: Stephen, a Greek man whose name literally meant: *"crowned."*[69]

This is the same imagery found in chapter five of the ancient apocryphal work entitled, the Wisdom of Solomon:

> But the righteous live for evermore; their reward also is with the Lord, and the care of them is with the most High. [16] Therefore shall they receive a glorious kingdom, and a beautiful crown from the Lord's hand: for with his right hand shall he cover them, and with his arm shall he protect them[70]

It's here in Ya'akov's letter that most commentaries point to the Greek "stephanos" or *crown* as referring to the Roman olympic games. This

---

66 D'etb'Char "ܝܘܚܒܬܐ " SEDRA3. Here used in the perfect tense.

67 See Harris, J. Rendel, "The Odes and Psalms of Solomon Published from the Syriac Version" pg. xxvii, where he states, "the baptized wore crowns. A reference to Hermas will show in early ritual was a controversy in the early Church of the West that there as to whether baptized people should be crowned or not, and it is decided in the negative, because the crown belongs properly to the Martyrs."

68 See Matthew 27:29

69 Thayer's Greek-English Lexicon of the New Testament, Stephanos: Stephen = "crowned"

70 The King James Version Apocrypha, (Oak Harbor, WA: Logos Research Systems, Inc.) 1995.

would be a mistake, however, because we know Ya'akov was a righteous Jew, living and writing from Jerusalem. On that point Jamieson, Fausset, and Brown point out,

> The "crown" here is not an allusion to the crown or garland given to winners in the games; for this, though a natural allusion for Paul in writing to the heathen, among whom such games existed, would be less appropriate for James in addressing the Jewish Christians, who regarded Gentile usages with aversion.[71]

The Aramaic used here is "kelila d'chayye." The "crown" or "kelila" was used to indicate: "*a crown; a completion of a building; the crown of betrothal (made from wreathes); a wedding, the nuptial rite; the crown of victory.*"[72]

What each of these examples share in common is that they are all complete. A crown is complete in that it is a circle. A building is made complete when it has the last bit of trim placed on it. A wedding is completed when the final vows are declared. The victory is made complete when the battle has finally ended. And it appears that Ya'akov's message may contain elements of all of these.

Think about it. He's been using the imagery of being made whole, lacking nothing, not lacking wisdom, not lacking stability, not doubting, not lacking a single-minded devotion. In this section Ya'akov has been pointing toward that which makes us ready for the One that we love, who loves us (active participle here). In fact, we are being made into a building fit for worship, and we are being made ready for the wedding, and we are, through the face of trials, being made complete, lacking in nothing.

Through trials we're prepared. By our endurance through those trials we are crowned for the approaching wedding day.

---

71 Robert Jamieson, A. R. Fausset and David Brown, A Commentary on the Old and New Testaments, notes on James 1:12
72 Payne Smith's A compendious Syriac Dictionary, pg. 216

> **James 1:13-16 MGI**   No one should say when he is
> tempted, "I am tempted by God," for God is not tempted
> with evil [things] and does not tempt anyone. (14) But each
> man is tempted by his [own] desire and he desires and is
> dragged away (15) and this desire conceives and produces
> sin. And sin, when it is matured, produces death. (16) Do
> not err, my beloved brothers.

Ya'akov is now discussing what is known as "yetzer hara" or "the
inclination of evil."

The Rabbis comment on this subject, saying:

> Today it says, do this; Tomorrow, worship an idol. The man goes
> and worships.[73]

And again:

> "Evil desire is, at the beginning, like the thread of a spider's web;
> afterwards it is like a cart rope."[74]

The Jewish Annotated New Testament notes:

> Rabbinic literature contains many references to *temptation* and
> the *evil desire*. For example, Babylonian Talmud Sukkot 52a
> compares the righteous winning their struggle against
> temptation to one who conquers a mountain; In Sukkot 52b it
> advises that one can melt and smash the evil urge by engaging in
> Torah study. God will help defeat it. Bava Batra 16b equates the
> "evil urge," "satan," and "the angel of death."[75]

---

73 Clarke, Adam, Commentary on the Bible, James 1:13 quoting Midrash hanaalam,
   fol. 20, and Yalcut Rubeni, fol. 17
74 Ibid., quoting Sanhedrin, fol. 99
75 Jewish Annotated New Testament, pg. 429

It's interesting that from a Jewish perspective, it's not the serpent that actually brings death to a person but rather it is the sin that he is enticed to perform which actually brings death.

The Jewish writing entitled, Sefer HaZohar tells us:

> "the concupiscent soul (or "lust") stirs up the evil figment, and imagines by it, and it cleaves to every evil imagination, שממתעברת, "until it conceives a little", and produces in the heart of man the evil thought, and cleaves to it; and as yet it is in his heart, and is not "finished" to do it, until this desire or lust stirs up the strength of the body, first to cleave to the evil figment, and then תשלום הרעה, "sin is finished"; as it is said, Gen_19:36."[76]

The psalmist got it right.

> **Psalms 141:4 ESV** Do not let my heart incline to any evil, to busy myself with wicked deeds in company with men who work iniquity, and let me not eat of their delicacies!

In this section, Ya'akov is describing sexual sin. Which by the way is what is normally meant by "yetzer hara." The evil inclination that is described here by Ya'akov is very specific.

- First, it is the "lust" or "desire" which tempts. (v.14)

- Then, it's the "lust" or "desire" which draws one away. (v.14)

- Finally, it's the "lust" or "desire" (v.15) which brings forth sin.

---

76 Gill, Ibid., James 1:16 Quoting from Midrash Haneelam in Zohar in Gen. fol. 67. 4.

> **v.15**   ...and this desire conceives and produces sin. And sin, when it is matured, produces death.

The end result of this "drawing away" is conception, birth, maturity and death. These are considered the four basic stages of life, but here it's the four stages of sin which bring death. Death, because the person is drawn away. Drawn away from what? Drawn away from Elohim. This is why Ya'akov can say:

> **v.16**   Do not err, my beloved brothers.

Never does Elohim tempt us to be "drawn away" from Himself!

The word here for "mistake" means to "wander, err, forget, deceive, astray, delude."[77] This is the same word that is used by Yeshua when He warns us, saying:

> **Luke 21:8 ESV**   And he said, "See that you are not *led astray*. For many will come in my name, saying, 'I am he!' and, 'The time is at hand!' Do not go after them."

Ya'akov is warning us to check our perspective regarding trials. He says that Elohim desires that we choose life for ourselves and not death. Remember that God has placed before each one of us the ability to choose. He says to us:

> **Deuteronomy 30:15-20 ESV**   "See, I have set before you today life and good, death and evil. (16) If you obey the commandments of the LORD your God that I command you today, by loving the LORD your God, by walking in his ways, and by keeping his commandments and his statutes and his rules, then you shall live and multiply, and the LORD your God

---

77 SEDRA3, "ܛܥܝܘܢ" "t'ethun"

will bless you in the land that you are entering to take possession of it. (17) But if your heart turns away, and you will not hear, but are drawn away to worship other gods and serve them, (18) I declare to you today, that you shall surely perish. You shall not live long in the land that you are going over the Jordan to enter and possess. (19) I call heaven and earth to witness against you today, that I have set before you life and death, blessing and curse. Therefore choose life, that you and your offspring may live, (20) loving the LORD your God, obeying his voice and holding fast to him, for he is your life and length of days, that you may dwell in the land that the LORD swore to your fathers, to Abraham, to Isaac, and to Jacob, to give them."

This is the same choice that was given to our first parents. Elohim instructed them to choose life, but instead they chose that which brought death and drew them away from God. They chose poorly. Their choice led ultimately to death. It led not only to their death, but the entire human race was consequently subjected to the reality of death.

The text in Genesis, which tells us all about the original temptation and the drawing away and separation from God, gives us great insights into the character of The Almighty.

> **Genesis 2:16 ESV** And the LORD God commanded the man, saying, "You may surely eat of every tree of the garden..."

This Hebrew verb translated as "commanded" describes how God instructed the man and the woman. This word is in what's known as the Piel stem, which means it was an ongoing continuous command, and not a one-time instruction. Not only was it continuous, but it was intense! The Creator wasn't merely issuing a mandate, but He was giving them repeated and emphatic instruction on the necessity of not eating that fruit! *"It's poison! It will kill you!"* And in reality, it did more than just kill them. Death of their physical selves would come as they breathed their last breath. But their choice brought them another more immediate consequence they did not anticipate: it drew them away from God. That is precisely Ya'akov's warning to us in this part of his message.

Enduring under temptation and trials draws us closer to God, as much as falling into temptation during trials draws us away.

> **James 1:17 MGI** Every good and complete gift [is] from above, coming down from the Father of lights, with whom there is not any inconstancy, not even a shadow of change.

Ya'akov is probably referring here to the words of the prophet Malachi:

Malachi 3:6 ESV "For I the LORD do not change; therefore you, O children of Jacob, are not consumed."

Unlike shadows, God doesn't change. The phrase, "Father of Lights," is a reference to Elohim who created the lights in the heavens. It is important to note that this phrase was commonly used in the Dead Sea Scrolls. And here is our reference from Genesis:

Genesis 1:14-16 ESV And God said, "Let there be lights in the expanse of the heavens to separate the day from the night. And let them be for signs and for seasons, and for days and years, (15) and let them be lights in the expanse of the heavens to give light upon the earth." And it was so. (16) And God made the two great lights – the greater light to rule the day and the lesser light to rule the night – and the stars.

Rabbi Chaninah, who lived during the first century, said:

"No evil thing comes down from above."[78]

---

78 As quoted in the Great NT Greek commentary, notes on James 1:17

> **James 1:18 MGI** It is he [who] desired and fathered us by the word of truthfulness that we would be the first [fruit] of his created [ones].

Once again, remembering that this letter is addressed to the Jewish population of the diaspora, let's try to understand these terms and their intent.

First, notice that Ya'akov is contrasting man's desires with God's desires. Man, left to himself, will follow lies, which will lead to the committing of sin, which will give birth to death. God, however, through "truth," gives "new birth," which leads us to become a "first-fruit." A first-fruit is that which is completely committed and dedicated to God. A first-fruit is the first of a crop which is set apart, dedicated solely to God. Therefore, these Jewish believers who were sown among the Gentiles were, in a sense, examples of what the rest of the crop would look like.

Those are an echo of Prophet Jeremiah's words:

> **Jeremiah 2:3 ESV** Israel was holy to the LORD, the first-fruits of his harvest..."

Rabbi Sha'ul affirmed this very thing:

> **Romans 8:22-23 Murdock** For we know, that all the creatures are groaning and travailing in pain unto this day. (23) And not only they, but we also in whom are the first fruits of the Spirit, we groan within ourselves, and look anxiously for the adoption of sons, the redemption of our bodies.

So, Ya'akov is reminding these Jewish believers that it has been God's plan all along to bring new life to His people through the Messiah to make Israel a first-fruit of all of those who would come later. This was to happen through the process of "new birth."

Yeshua discusses this "new birth" with Nakdimon Ben Gurion

(Nicodemus) in the gospel of John:

> **John 3:3 Murdock** Jesus replied, and said to him: Verily, verily, I say to you, That, unless a man be born anew, he cannot behold the kingdom of God.

To be "born anew" or "born again" is actually a rabbinic term used for a gentile who undergoes a formal conversion to Judaism. The Talmud says:

> "One who has become a proselyte is like a child newly born."[79]

This wise leader is telling his brethren, "God has done something unique among us. Like Gentiles being born into Judaism, we Jews have also received a new start – by recognizing that the Messiah has come, and by receiving His Spirit."

---

79 Talmud – Mas. Yevamoth 22a

Chapter 6

In our previous chapter, we discussed Ya'akov's teaching about the results we will attain if we stand up under temptation, and the consequences for succumbing to them.

To make his point, Ya'akov used the imagery of fornication, and the child that it produces which leads to death. In an indirect way, by choosing to use this example, this is evidence that this wise old sage didn't try to avoid public criticism by being "politically correct."

In the Babylonian Talmud, we find a story which reflects the gossip of the day. This is a section that was contained within it's footnotes:

> In the uncensored text this passage follows: Was he then the son of Stada: surely he was the son of Pandira?-Said R. Hisda: The husband was Stada, the paramour was Pandira. But the husband was Pappos b. Judah? — His mother was Stada. But his mother was Miriam the hairdresser? — It is as we say in Pumbeditha: This one has been unfaithful to (lit., 'turned away from' — satath da) her husband.[80]

The common accusation of the day was that Miryam had been unfaithful to Yosef by having intercourse with a Roman guard named "Pandira," and that as a consequence of their sin, Miryam gave birth to a son who was then destined for destruction. This, of course, is the type

---

80 BabylonianTalmud, Mas Shabbat 104b, footnote 19 (Soncino edition); Friedrich August Nitzsch (1840) suggested that the name "Pandira" may refer to a panther being a lustful animal and thus have the meaning of "whore", additionally being a pun on parthenos meaning virgin. See: Wikipedia's article "Pandira" which quotes Schäfer, Peter (2007). Jesus in the Talmud (3rd ed.). Princeton, New Jersey: Princeton University Press.

of illustration one avoids *if* there's any truth to the accusation. However, Ya'akov uses this very scenario as an example for not yielding under temptation! It is quite obvious, since Ya'akov refers to Yeshua by the Divine Name of "MarYah" (the Aramaic form of YHVH), that he considers himself to be serving Elohim Himself,[81] and believes these accusations to be completely without merit. If my premise is correct, then it makes the following section very interesting indeed. It's here that Ya'akov transitions from using an example of gossip (that he would have known well and that would have had a direct impact on his family) to discussing what comes from the use of careless words and uncontrolled anger.

> **James 1:19 MGI** And you, my beloved brothers, everyone of you should be quick to hear and slow to speak and slow to be angry.

Here he is invoking a commonly known adage of the day. For example, in the Mishnah Avoth we read:

> Shammai used to say: Make thy study of the Torah a matter of established regularity; speak little, but do much; and receive all men with a pleasant countenance.[82]

In the Talmud we find another section of commentary concerning publicly hearing the words of the Torah:

> Be swift to hear them: slow to speak.[83]

Here, in a similar fashion, Ya'akov combines the elements of listening, speaking, and acting along with the practice of studying Torah.
He continues to spell it out to us for four more verses:

---

81 Not to mention the fact that Ya'akov uses the masculine pronoun in this example.
82 Mishnah Avoth, 1.15 (Soncino edition)
83 Gill's notes on James 1:19 where he quotes the gloss. in the Babylonian Talmud, Megilla, fol. 21. 1. ,

James 1:22 Murdock   But be ye doers of the word, and not hearers only; and do not deceive yourselves.

Here the Aramaic term for "word"[84] indicates that which is spoken (it implies that which is read aloud from the bimah).

It's obvious here that Ya'akov is reminding his Jewish brothers to pay attention, and be mindful to act upon what they're hearing in the synagogue.

Now, that we have a better idea of the background, let's go back and read this section as a whole.

> **James 1:19-25 MGI**   And you, my beloved brothers, everyone of you should be quick to hear and slow to speak and slow to be angry. (20) For the anger of man does not serve the justification of God. (21) Because of this, put away from you all uncleanness and the abundance of wickedness and receive with meekness the word that is implanted in our nature that is able to give life to your souls. (22) And be doers of the word and not hearers only and do not deceive yourselves. (23) For if anyone is a hearer of the word and not a doer of it, this [one] is like him who sees his face in a mirror, (24) for he sees himself and passes on and forgets what kind [of man] he was. (25) And everyone who looks into the fulfilled law of liberty and remains in it is not a hearer of a report that is forgotten, but a doer of deeds. And this [one] will be blessed in his deed.

There's a lot going on here in this text. First, let's make sure that we don't miss the comparison between the subject of "anger" in verses nineteen and twenty, with the words of Yeshua in the sermon on the mount.

---

84 SEDRA3 "ܡܠܬܐ" Payne Smith's Syriac Dictionary defines this as: "verbal of words." pg. 278

Yeshua said this about anger:

> **Matthew 5:22 ESV**   But I say to you that everyone who is angry with his brother will be liable to judgment; whoever insults his brother will be liable to the council; and whoever says, 'You fool!' will be liable to the hell of fire.

Yeshua teaches that it is the anger inside that produces the outward action which results in murder. So anger, according to Yeshua, is very serious when it's not dealt with. Ya'akov agrees. He describes anger as "defiling"[85] a person. And it's this very word that Ya'akov used to describe defilement through fornication, defilement through the act of *deflowering* a woman, defilement through pagan rituals, and defilement through idolatry.

That is, Ya'akov instructs us to, in the midst of the temptation which draws us away (with the goal of defiling us), stop, listen, and apply God's Torah!

> **v.21** Because of this, put away from you all uncleanness and the abundance of wickedness and receive with meekness the word that is implanted in our nature that is able to give life to your souls.

When we take the time to read through the Aramaic text we find that it is unlike any of it's Greek counterparts.

The phrase "in our nature" is nowhere to be found among the Greek manuscripts. This is significant, in that it points to the source being Aramaic, and not Greek. More than that, it's message is significant! Ya'akov is saying that by receiving God's Word into our lives it becomes part of our very nature!

---

85 See "ܬܢܦܘܬܐ," "Tanp'uta" Payne Smith, Ibid., pg. 177

73

Ya'akov paints a picture. This picture shows the Torah as being like a seed that has been planted into the very nature of a person. And through that implantation, the person's very soul is resurrected.

Rabbi Sha'ul uses this same agricultural imagery when he refers to this Torah seed as the "nourishing root" into which the gentile believers are "grafted."

> **Romans 11:16-17 ESV**   If the dough offered as first-fruits is holy, so is the whole lump, and if the root is holy, so are the branches. (17) But if some of the branches were broken off, and you, although a wild olive shoot, were grafted in among the others and now share in the nourishing root of the olive tree...

What is the nourishing root? It is, of course, Judaism – the system for, and the practice of, following the Torah!

Most translations use the Greek word "sozo" for "root," which means "*to save*," but the original Aramaic translates root as "*to make alive*" or "*to resurrect*." This is used to describe the quickening, or the restoring of life. It is also the same word used for the resurrection of the Messiah from the grave.

Ya'akov is saying that when the teachings in the Torah are followed, they will bring new life to the one who follows, resurrected life! This term affirms our connection to the resurrected Messiah, who is Himself, God's Word and the Living Torah – the One who overcame all of life's temptations! Ya'akov continues...

> **v.22**   And be doers of the word and not hearers only and do not deceive yourselves.

King David put it this way:

> **Psalms 103:17-18 ESV**   But the steadfast love of the LORD is from everlasting to everlasting on those who fear him, and his

righteousness to children's children, (18) to those who *keep his covenant and remember to do his commandments.*

This is the reason that God has given His instructions to us. It is His desire that we should follow them. He wants us to live, really live. He desires that we live the lives that He intended for us to experience. I think that there's a mental block for many of us which inhibits us from appropriately understanding our faith and it's essential connection to action. On this subject, the Master said:

> **Matthew 7:21-27 ESV** Not everyone who says to me, 'Lord, Lord,' will enter the kingdom of heaven, but the one who does the will of my Father who is in heaven. (22) On that day many will say to me, 'Lord, Lord, did we not prophesy in your name, and cast out demons in your name, and do many mighty works in your name?' (23) And then will I declare to them, 'I never knew you; depart from me, you workers of lawlessness.' (24) Everyone then who hears these words of mine and does them will be like a wise man who built his house on the rock. (25) And the rain fell, and the floods came, and the winds blew and beat on that house, but it did not fall, because it had been founded on the rock. (26) And everyone who hears these words of mine and does not do them will be like a foolish man who built his house on the sand. (27) And the rain fell, and the floods came, and the winds blew and beat against that house, and it fell, and great was the fall of it.

In other words, obedience is the essential ingredient for a healthy faith.

Ya'akov, in his imagination, now scans through the faces in all of the Jewish congregations, seeing men and women who have spent the better part of each Shabbat chanting, praying, and listening to the text for years. Then he says to them:

> **vs. 23-24**   For if anyone is a hearer of the word and not a doer of it, this [one] is like him who sees his face in a mirror, (24) for he sees himself and passes on and forgets what kind [of man] he was.

Put into practice what God says to do! You *hear* the "shema" each week,[86] now make sure you're also *doing*!

Gill's notes on this section are insightful:

> The Arabic version here again reads, "a hearer of the law", and so some copies; not hearing, but practice, is the main thing; not theory, but action: hence, says R. Simeon, not the word, or the searching into it, and the explanation of it, is the root, or principal thing, אלא המעשה, "but the work" (Pirke Abot 1.17): and if a man is only a preacher, or a hearer, and not a doer.[87]

The Babylonian Talmud declares:

> R. Joshua B. Karha said: Whosoever studies the Torah and does not revise it is likened unto one who sows without reaping. R. Joshua said: He who studies the Torah and then forgets it is like a woman who bears [a child] and buries [it.] R. Akiba said: 'Chant it every day, chant it every day.'[88]

Rabbi Chanina once said:

> If one's thoughts were of greater focus than one's deeds, the former would eventually perish.[89]

---

86 Lit., it's "be a shema-er"
87 Gill, notes on James 1:23
88 Babylonian Talmud, Sanhedrin 99a (Soncino edition)
89 The Jewish Annotated New Testament, pg 430 quoting Hanina ben Dosa from Avot de R. Natan A 22.2.

References to this biblical theme are too numerous throughout ancient Judaism for me to begin to do it justice here. It would be quite easy for me to site examples of the necessity of acting upon one's faith from each and every book of the Bible.

I will give just one quick example from the book of Jonah:

> **Jonah 3:10 ESV**   When God saw what they *did*, how they turned from their evil way, God relented of the disaster that he had said he would do to them, and he did not do it.

Authentic biblical faith takes action, works, deeds, involvement, responsibility, growth, discipleship and accountability!

> **v. 25**   And everyone who looks into the fulfilled law of liberty and remains in it is not a hearer of a report that is forgotten, but a doer of deeds. And this [one] will be blessed in his deed.

David Stern, commenting on this passage, says:

"God tests faith by the Word, not by man's words."

Why is this statement true? The Torah is perfect! It's this miraculous set of instructions that give us freedom when we follow them. Nevertheless, for centuries Christians have been taught that being "free from the Law" gives freedom.[90] According to Ya'akov, the opposite is true. Living by God's perfect instructions brings freedom! Ya'akov writes that through one's actions/works will one receive a blessing!

---

90 This is an incorrect interpretation of Rabbi Sha'ul's words in Romans 8:2. In this passage, Sha'ul is pointing out that it's the Torah that defines the sin in ourselves that brings death. God's instructions bring life, when we disregard them the result is death as described within the pages of Torah.

Yeshua said:

> **Matthew 5:19 ESV** Therefore whoever relaxes one of the least of these commandments and teaches others to do the same will be called least in the kingdom of heaven, but whoever does them and teaches them will be called great in the kingdom of heaven.

This term here in Matthew translated as "relaxes" is also used to describe an eagle as it loosens the prey from his talons in order to eat it. Therefore, "d'neshroa" can also be translated as *"eagle; loosen; lodge; begin; loosened, be loosened; eat, eat a meal."*[91]

God wants us to receive His blessing. He wants us to live blessed lives. This is why He calls us to obedience and to action, not to disregarding His instructions that actually bring us to a great life!

We finished this section with this instruction from Ya'akov:

> **James 1:26 MGI** And if a man supposes that he serves God and he does not hold his tongue, but the heart of this [man] deceives him, [then] his service is unprofitable.

Jewish wisdom literature constantly discusses the need to curb and control the tongue. Here are a couple of examples from the writings of David:

> **Psalm 34:13 ESV** Keep your tongue from evil, your lips from speaking lies.

> **Psalm 141:3 ESV** Set a guard, LORD, before my mouth, a gatekeeper at my lips.

---

91 SEDRA3, "d'neshroa"

> **James 1:27 MGI**   For the service that is pure and holy before God the Father is this, to visit orphans and widows in their troubles and to keep oneself without spot from the world.

About this, the Prophet Isaiah writes:

> **Isaiah 1:16-17 ESV**   Wash yourselves; make yourselves clean; remove the evil of your deeds from before my eyes; cease to do evil, (17) learn to do good; seek justice, correct oppression; bring justice to the fatherless, plead the widow's cause.

Let me conclude this chapter with a section from the Pirke Avot (The Sayings of the Fathers).

Chapter 5, verse 20, says:

> "There are four kinds of men who visit the synagogues,
>   1.   He who enters but does not work.
>   2.   He who works but does not enter.
>   3.   He who enters and works.
>   4.   He who neither enters nor works.
> The first two are indifferent characters; the third is the righteous man; the fourth is wholly evil."[92]

Do, do, do! Act, act, act! Assist the Lord in changing the world by allowing Him to change you! This is the whole content of chapter one.

If Ya'akov were speaking to us today, I believe he would remind us that, *A confession of belief without compassionate action is the mark of a corrupt religion.*

---

92 As quoted in Adam Clarke's Commentary on the book of James.

Chapter 7

As we continue and in order to understand the context of what Ya'akov is going to be talking about next, we need to take a trip to one of Yeshua's favorite places – a place He stayed, slept, and taught – the town of Capernaum. The entire second chapter surrounds the setting of the first-century setting, practice, and use of the synagogue.

> **James 2:1 MGI** My brothers, do not hold to the faith of the glory of our Lord Jesus Christ with respect of persons.

Ya'akov starts off this chapter with a very familiar Jewish image. One which would be prominent within the Jewish synagogue: the presence of God. Each local synagogue was used at least three times each week. It was at the synagogue that God's Word, His covenant with His people, would be spoken aloud, commented on, and practiced by the community. As Ya'akov begins talking about the local synagogues, he makes sure that He presents the presence of God as being there first.

He uses the phrase, *"the faith of the glory of our Lord (Master) Jesus Christ (Y'shua HaMashiyach)."* This term "glory" here is of major importance within the context of this passage and for our understanding of the Messiah.

If you recall, at the very beginning of the gospel accounts we see Sh'mon haTzaddik (Simon the Righteous) at the temple immediately after the circumcision of the Messiah, and he is pronouncing a b'rakhah (blessing) over Him. He says:

Luke 2:29-32 ESV "Lord, now you are letting your servant depart in peace, according to your word; (30) for my eyes have seen your salvation (31) that you have prepared in the presence of all peoples, (32) a light for revelation to the Gentiles, and for *glory* to your people Israel."

It's this word "glory" that is significant. It is the word used to express none other than the Shekinah, or presence, of God. The word "shekinah" literally means: "*to dwell*." The Messiah was to be the shekinah or "dwelling presence" of God. It was thought that where two or more were gathered to discuss the words of the Torah, that God's shekinah would be present.

Pirke Avoth 3.3 says:

> "Rabbi Chananiah ben Teradyon said, Two that sit together and are occupied in words of Torah have the Shekinah among them."

Now, compare that to Yeshua's words from Matthew:

> **Matthew 18:20 CJB** For wherever two or three are assembled in my name, I am there with them.

The writer of Hebrews declares:

> **Hebrews 1:3 CJB** This Son is the radiance of the Sh'khinah, the very expression of God's essence, upholding all that exists by his powerful word; and after he had, through himself, made purification for sins, he sat down at the right hand of HaG'dulah BaM'romim (the Power on high).

In every synagogue, the central part is the presence of the Torah. By speaking about the synagogues, Ya'akov reminds believers of the Living Torah's presence, existing there through the Messiah.

> **James 2:2-4 MGI** For if a man should enter your assembly with rings of gold or with beautiful garments and a poor man should enter with filthy garments, (3) and you look at that one clothed with beautiful garments and say to him, "Sit here [in] a good [place]," and to the poor man you say, "Stand back or sit here before the footstool," (4) behold, are you not discriminating among yourselves and have you [not] become expounders of evil reasonings? showing double mindedness among yourselves and becoming advocates of evil thoughts?

At first glance, this passage seems pretty clear. It has to do with preference given for social status. In other words, he warned against wealthy people in a synagogue being treated better than the poor. But, what Ya'akov is saying here goes far deeper than that.

Synagogues during the first century were the primary gathering places for the Jewish community. In fact, this is what both the Hebrew word "synagogue," and the Aramaic word "sunagoge," means: *a gathering.*

Jews were typically in synagogue on Monday, Thursday and Shabbat. Mondays and Thursdays would not only be used for daily prayer, but for various other uses as well. The synagogue served as the local school house (beit midrash = house of study), and served as the place where the Beit Din (the Jewish court system, literally, the House of Judgment) would gather to decide public matters and civil disputes. *"He stole my goat!"* *"She charged me too much for that jar!"*

Let me share with you some of the rules of the Jewish court system to see if any of this sounds like Ya'akov's letter.

> "two adversaries [at law with each other], if one of them is clothed "with precious garments", ("goodly apparel",) and the other is clothed with "vile raiment", [the judge] says to the honorable person, either clothe him as you are, while you are contending with him, or be clothed as he is, that you may be

alike, or on an equal footing."[93]
- (Maimonides. Hilchot Sanhedrin, c. 21. sect. 2.)

And this section from the Talmud,

> "one shall not sit, and another stand, but both shall stand; but if
> the sanhedrim, or court, please to let them sit, they sit; but one
> does not sit above, and the other below; but one by the side of
> the other."[94]
> - (Maimon. ib. sect. 3. vid. T. Bab. Shavuot, fol. 30. 1.)

Both of these examples are exact illustrations for Ya'akov's greater lesson
here. He is pointing out to his Jewish brothers that they need to take a
lesson from the legal system that brings justice. He's admonishing them
for treating each other worse in this building on the Sabbath than the
legal system does in the same building during the week. He's saying that
administrators of justice have a better sense of morality in the synagogue
while they're serving the community than the congregation does when
claiming to be serving God.

The instructions are clear: don't show contempt for one and favor
towards the other based on what you think they'll contribute (remember
that everything in the synagogue was donated). Ya'akov says we are not
to see the community of worship with secular eyes.

> **v.1** My brothers, do not hold to the faith of the glory of our
> Lord Jesus Christ with respect of persons.

The fourth verse is Ya'akov's conclusion to the instruction which he
posed in the first:

---

93 Gill's commentary notes on James 2:2
94 Ibid., James 2:3

> **v.4** ...are you not discriminating among yourselves and have you [not] become expounders of evil reasonings? showing double mindedness among yourselves and becoming advocates of evil thoughts?

In short, his instructions are:

Make sure that you don't act unrighteous because the Messiah's presence is here, His glory is here with you in the synagogue, this place where you say that you worship Him, this place where you read about Him, and study about Him, the very place where during the week your children are learning about God's justice! Make sure then that you are acting justly.

> **James 2:5 MGI** Hear, my beloved brothers, was it not the poor of the world, but [who are] rich in faith [that] God chose to be heirs in the kingdom that God promised to those who love him?

"The poor of the world"[95] was a very common phrase. It was used to distinguish "the poor of Israel" from "the poor from the nations." That makes this section even more special for us.

Here, we can see that the first leader of this messianic Jewish movement (even when he's addressing the Jewish community), had his eyes and heart on the gentiles that were becoming a part of the coming kingdom. Notice that Ya'akov makes this clear as he distinguishes the Messiah's Kingdom as that which was promised to those who "love Him."

The word for love here is "D'ramyin" = "ܕܪܚܡܝܢ" and is the same word used for the command to "love our neighbor as ourself." This word is an active participle, meaning that it's present action. It comes from the Aramaic term for *womb.* Therefore, this word indicates a love which

---

95 See Babylonian Talmud Gittin, 30a

84

demonstrates: *compassion, care, hospitality, and trusting friendship.*[96] This is the characteristic of those who are true heirs of the Kingdom.

Notice that Ya'akov calls the gentiles "the poor of the world." Then, he says that they're rich in what counts in the Kingdom, which is faith. Does this mean all gentiles were poor? Of course not! It means they were poor in faith towards God because they didn't yet have the Torah. The Lord showed compassion on them and they became rich in faith and heirs of the kingdom. This section has presented a two-fold message.

1. Instruction against favoritism in the synagogue.

2. Instruction to the Jews on how they should treat the gentile believers who were coming into the synagogues to worship God.

We see these instructions evoked once again by Ya'akov as recorded in the book of Acts. What's the topic? Gentiles coming to faith and visiting the synagogues, of course.

> **Acts 15:19-21 ESV** Therefore my judgment is that we should not trouble those of the Gentiles who turn to God, (20) but should write to them to abstain from the things polluted by idols, and from sexual immorality, and from what has been strangled, and from blood. (21) For from ancient generations Moses has had in every city those who proclaim him, for he is read every Sabbath in the synagogues."

---

96 See Payne Smith pg. 537

Ya'akov concludes his thought with these words:

> **James 2:6-9 MGI**   But you have rejected the poor. Behold, do not rich [men] elevate themselves over you and drag you to court? (7) Behold, do they not reproach the good name that was called on you? (8) And if you fulfill the law of God in this, as it is written: YOU SHOULD LOVE YOUR NEIGHBOR AS YOURSELF, you are doing well. (9) But if you are respecting persons, you commit sin and you are reproved by the law as transgressors of the law.

It was the wealthy folks who, for the most part, funded the synagogues. They were also, predominantly, the same ones that came against the proclamation that Yeshua was the Messiah.

So to them, Ya'akov says: *"Why are you favoring the wealthy? They despise His worthy name! Instead, care for all believers with no thought of their social standing. By this you fulfill God's command of love in the Torah (His instruction manual)."*

Chapter 8

Now, in our text Ya'akov continues with his instructions for doing the right thing, treating people fairly, judging appropriately – with the familiar admonition to love your neighbor as yourself. This is actually a direct quote from the Torah:

> **Leviticus 19:18 ESV**   You shall not take vengeance or bear a grudge against the sons of your own people, but you shall love your neighbor as yourself: I am the LORD.

It was specifically repeated by the Messiah when He shared the main intention of the Torah:

> **Mark 12:29-31 ESV**   Jesus answered, "The most important is, 'Hear, O Israel: The Lord our God, the Lord is one. (30) And you shall love the Lord your God with all your heart and with all your soul and with all your mind and with all your strength.' (31) The second is this: 'You shall love your neighbor as yourself.' There is no other commandment greater than these."

Ya'akov goes on to make his point by explaining that when you break any aspect of God's instruction, you have broken the whole thing. It's for this reason we can't just pick and choose what we think might be the most important part. We must simply do what God says to do.

> **James 2:10 MGI**   For he who keeps the whole law and offends in one [thing] is found guilty of the whole law.

The term "keep" is the Aramaic term, "netar." It's primary meaning is three-fold:

    (1) *to guard, keep, protect, restrain*
    (2) *to reserve, store, preserve*
    (3) *to take care of, observe, watch*[97]

This is contrasted by the Aramaic word for "offends," which in Ya'akov's language was:"shera" which means:

    (1) *to slip, stumble*
    (2) *to offend, transgress*
    (3) *to falter*[98]

The evident contrast is between the "guarding, protecting, and watching" of the Torah, which keeps one from sin, and the "slipping, stumbling, or faltering" which represents the commission of sin.

This is all most certainly reminiscent of what Yeshua had preached:

> **Matthew 5:18-19 ESV**   For truly, I say to you, until heaven and earth pass away, not an iota, not a dot, will pass from the Law until all is accomplished. (19) Therefore whoever relaxes one of the least of these commandments and teaches others to do the same will be called least in the kingdom of heaven, but whoever does them and teaches them will be called great in the kingdom of heaven.

Of course, this was based upon the same teaching in the Torah:

> **Deuteronomy 27:26 ESV**   'Cursed be anyone who does not confirm the words of this law by doing them.' And all the people shall say, 'Amen.'

---

97 SEDRA3 ܢܛܪ

98 SEDRA3 ܫܪܐ

The rabbinical interpretation of the day can be summed up in this discussion from the Talmud:

> If [it be suggested that it is] in agreement with that of R. Meir who holds that a person who is suspected of disregarding one matter [of law] is held suspect in regard to all the Torah, the statement should also apply to any of the other prohibitions of the Torah...[99]

Our verse tells us that Ya'akov agrees.

> **James 2:10 ESV** For he that will *keep* the whole Torah and yet *fail* in one aspect of it, is an enemy to the whole Torah.

Next, Ya'akov gives examples of this "failing."

> **James 2:11 MGI** For he who said: DO NOT COMMIT ADULTERY, said, DO NOT KILL. Now if you do not commit adultery, but you kill, you have become a transgressor of the law.

When you slow down, this quotation in Ya'akov is a bit interesting. First, it comes originally from Exodus 20:13-14, which says:

> **Exodus 20:13-14 ESV** You shall not murder. (14) You shall not commit adultery.

And this is precisely what it's retelling in Deuteronomy. Here it is:

> **Deuteronomy 5:17-18 ESV** (17) You shall not murder. (18) And you shall not commit adultery.

But, did you notice that when Ya'akov quotes he reverses the order of

---

99 Babylonian Talmud, Mas. Eiruvin 69a (Soncino Edition)

the commandments? And Rabbi Sha'ul does precisely the same thing in speaking to the Romans,

> **Romans 13:9 ESV** For the commandments, "You shall not commit adultery, You shall not murder, You shall not steal, You shall not covet," and any other commandment, are summed up in this word: "You shall love your neighbor as yourself."

So, what gives? Let's continue in our text for now and we'll answer that question in our next chapter.

Our author says that by the breaking of one commandment one becomes a "defiler of Torah." This was a well-known Aramaic idiom of the day, denoting one who is trying to get away with something. The phrase is "avar al." It can be translated as: "*a turning against; a turning away from; a crossing over a prohibited boundary*;" or even as "*a going around something marked off.*"[100]

Each of the instructions found in God's word points us towards how to live free. When we break His instructions, we demonstrate the inability to live as free people. We are in a very real way then, slaves to sin, living within the chains of spiritual bondage.

> **James 2:12 MGI** So speak and so act, as people who are going to be judged by the law of liberty.

The Lord desires that we live free! Ya'akov is trying to help us do just that. He is telling us that when we break just one of the commands, it's like removing an essential element for life. In other words, a man may have food, but deprived of oxygen, he would still die. Or he may have oxygen, but without water, he's dead meat!

---

100 See entry "ܥܒܪ " Aramaic Peshitta New Testament Database (APNT), Copyright © 2005 by Janet M. Magiera.

It's the same with God's principles for life. Every one is essential. Each one is vital. And when we choose not to live by them, we are in essence, choosing to live in bondage.

Rabbi Sha'ul said:

> **Romans 8:19-21 ESV** For the creation waits with eager longing for the revealing of the sons of God. (20) For the creation was subjected to futility, not willingly, but because of him who subjected it, in hope (21) that the creation itself will be set free from its bondage to corruption and obtain the freedom of the glory of the children of God.

> **James 2:13 MGI** For judgment will be without mercy on that one who has not practiced mercy. By mercy, you will be elevated above judgment.

What one has practiced in life is what one will receive in the life to come. This concept is very commonly found in the writings of the first-century Jewish community. It only makes sense that we find it here in the writings of Ya'akov, as well.

The Babylonian Talmud has recorded:

> For in all the measures [of punishment or reward] taken by the Holy One, blessed be He, the Divine act befits the [human] deed.[101]

I like the way that Bauscher has translated the Aramaic text here:

> **Vs 13** For the judgment is without mercy against him who does not practice mercy; with mercy you have dominion over judgment.[102]

---

101 Mas. Sanhedrin, 90a (Soncino Edition)
102 Bauscher, Glenn David – The Peshitta Aramaic-English New Testament and

91

Or, as the Ethiopian version translates it:

> He only shall glory in the day of judgment, who has shown mercy.

Once again, we see the invisible threads of thought which connect Ya'akov to the words of Yeshua. And the Jewish idea of "measure for measure" is no exception.

> **Matthew 5:7 ESV**　Blessed are the merciful, for they shall receive mercy.

> **Matthew 6:14 ESV**　or if you forgive others their trespasses, your heavenly Father will also forgive you,

Yeshua's ancestor, David, said the very same thing:

> **2 Samuel 22:26-27 ESV**　With the merciful you show yourself merciful; with the blameless man you show yourself blameless; (27) with the purified you deal purely, and with the crooked you make yourself seem tortuous.

In Judaism, this is known as "midah ke neged midah" or "*measure for measure.*"

Ya'akov says that mercy is greater than harshness, but one must practice it, live by it, do it. And in the practice and lifestyle of mercy (chesed) one becomes more in-line with the character and mercy (chesed) of God.

David would also write:

> **Psalms 62:12 ESV**　..and that to you, O Lord, belongs steadfast love. For you will render to a man according to his work.

Interlinear Translation, Lulu Publishing

God will give to man what he deserves, but if we practice mercy, not only will we receive mercy in return, we become more like Him!

> **James 2:14 MGI**   What is the profit, my brothers, if someone says, "I have faith," and has no works? Is his faith able to give him life?

This is now the beginning of a hard look at the topic of faith from Jewish eyes! We will now begin an examination of our relationship with God. What is the basis and foundation for our connection and relationship with God? And how can a person truly know that they have it? Is there actually some way to quantify it?

Ya'akov's answer to these questions is: "*Yes you can! You can know if you truly have a connection with God, that you have 'faith' in God by these evidences!*"

> **James 2:15-17 MGI**   And if a brother or a sister should be naked and lacking food for the day (16) and one of you says to them, "Go in peace, be warm and be satisfied," and you do not give them what is necessary for the body, what is the profit? (17) So also, faith alone without works is dead.

emunah (which we defined in earlier chapters as: "firm action") without action is dead. In other words, how can a characteristic which has within its very nature action, exist without having action in it's very nature? It can't! Without action, it would cease to be faith, cease to exist, cease to have life. It would be dead!

Once again, we're forced to go back to the teaching of Yeshua. Here, He told a story very much like the illustration that we just read:

> **Matthew 25:34-46 ESV**   Then the King will say to those on his right, 'Come, you who are blessed by my Father, inherit the

kingdom prepared for you from the foundation of the world. (35) For I was hungry and you *gave* me food, I was thirsty and you *gave* me drink, I was a stranger and you *welcomed* me, (36) I was naked and you *clothed* me, I was sick and you <u>visited</u> me, I was in prison and you *came* to me.' (37) Then the righteous will answer him, saying, 'Lord, when did we see you hungry and feed you, or thirsty and give you drink? (38) And when did we see you a stranger and welcome you, or naked and clothe you? (39) And when did we see you sick or in prison and visit you?' (40) And the King will answer them, 'Truly, I say to you, as you *did it* to one of the least of these my brothers, you *did it* to me.' (41) "Then he will say to those on his left, 'Depart from me, you cursed, into the eternal fire prepared for the devil and his angels. (42) For I was hungry and you *gave me no food,* I was thirsty and you *gave me no drink,* (43) I was a stranger and you *did not welcome me,* naked and you *did not clothe me,* sick and in prison and you *did not visit me.*' (44) Then they also will answer, saying, 'Lord, when did we see you hungry or thirsty or a stranger or naked or sick or in prison, and did not minister to you?' (45) Then he will answer them, saying, 'Truly, I say to you, as you *did not do* it to one of the least of these, you *did not do* it to me.' (46) And these will go away into eternal punishment, but the righteous into eternal life."

Take notice of how many times we find the words which communicate to *"do it," "did it,"* or to have *"done it."* This parable of living this life and the coming judgment is about action! The two groups are separated by either words or deeds. One group is seen as merely having *said* this or that. The other group is accepted because they *did* this or that. As we have already seen, faith without action is mere philosophy, and philosophies do not equal salvation. In the same way, thinking doesn't always equal having. A person can think all that they want, but it doesn't necessarily make the thought a reality. Biblical faith is not a philosophy we believe. It is a system of relationship between concrete facts and concrete actions. These two are inseparable, and it takes both for an authentic biblical faith.

> **James 2:18-20 MGI** For a man will say to you, "You have faith," and to me, "I have works." Show me your faith without works and I will show you my faith by my works. (19) You believe that God is one. You do well! Even the demons believe and tremble. (20) Now do you want to understand, oh frail man, that faith without works is dead?

The term "works" is a Jewish term synonymous with "good deeds" or "mitzvot."

We're told here that the person who isn't doing works are to be compared to the fallen angels because they share the same "faith" or "belief system." Both the person without works and the demons have an "understanding" or a "faith/belief," but it does not produce life. Therefore, it is a dead belief because it is a faith void of good works. The demons have an understanding of God, but they do not follow Him. In the same way, the person who has an understanding of God but does not take action through good works or deeds is not actually following Him either!

This is Ya'akov's point: If you truly are following Him, you'll do what He says to do. If you don't do what He says, then you have the same type of faith as the demons. To be clear, what about the person who says they believe but isn't living-out their faith? According to Ya'akov, they're floating in the same boat as the demons. Both are lost and separated from God, which equals being dead, because both are in disobedience to God.

Here, Ya'akov's message stands in sharp contrast to today's philosophical Christian approach to God, where faith is synonymous with understanding, but very distant from our actions. Ya'akov, though, sees them as being inseparable.

Next, Ya'akov gives us a picture of what true faith looks like as he borrows from the Father of our faith, Abraham.

95

> **James 2:21-24 MGI** Was not our father Abraham justified by works when he offered Isaac his son on the altar? (22) You see that his faith aided his works and [that] by works, his faith was matured. (23) And the scripture was fulfilled that said: ABRAHAM BELIEVED IN GOD AND IT WAS COUNTED TO HIM FOR JUSTIFICATION, and he was called the friend of God. (24) You see that by works a man is justified and not by faith alone.

Abraham acted upon His understanding of God's directions for His life. God spoke it. Abraham did it. Faith! This is what Ya'akov means when he says it "aided his works" and "rendered it complete." It was because of Abraham's follow-through that God considered him to be righteous.

> **Question #1:** If God had only *contemplated* the act on Calvary, would that have been enough to save humanity?

> **Question #2:** If God had merely *believed* that He could save humanity, would that have been enough to save humanity?

> **Question #3:** If Yeshua had *wished* that He could have given His life for humanity, would that have been the same as Him actually saving humanity?

The answer to all three questions is: *No, absolutely not!*

Like Abraham, God has called us into action! This, for us, means putting our understanding of what He wants accomplished into motion. We must *do* something in the real world, not just consider doing something in a philosophical one.

Chapter 9

In the previous chapter, we discovered a reversal between a text in Exodus and a quoted text in Deuteronomy. Let's take another look at that to ensure that we understand what's going on.

> **James 2:11 MGI** For he who said: DO NOT COMMIT ADULTERY, said, DO NOT KILL. Now if you do not commit adultery, but you kill, you have become a transgressor of the law.

Our author is quoting from the book of Deuteronomy, and I'd like to walk you through how I reached that conclusion. Originally, this set of commands came from the giving of the Torah at Mount Sinai. This event was recorded in Exodus (Sh'mot).

Here's how the text reads:

> **Exodus 20:13-14 ESV** You shall not murder. (14) You shall not commit adultery.

Notice that they're listed in the opposite order as in Ya'akov's letter.

Now, when we turn to the book of Deuteronomy (D'varim), the list of commandments are given again (thus the Greek title for the book, which means "the second law"). Here they are:

> **Deuteronomy 5:17-18 ESV_** You shall not murder. (18) And you shall not commit adultery.

Maybe you're thinking, *"Wait a minute! That's the same order as was given in the book of Exodus."* If you were, you would be right, and also wrong. You'd be correct in saying that our translation shows it to us this way, but also incorrect in that not every manuscript lists it the same. And this is how we know for sure that Ya'akov is quoting from Deuteronomy. It is also one more indication of why Deuteronomy was considered so important to the first-century Jewish community. Ya'akov is not the only one who quotes it in this order.

> **Luke 18:20 ESV**   You know the commandments: 'Do not commit adultery, Do not murder, Do not steal, Do not bear false witness, Honor your father and mother.'"

Here in Matthew, Yeshua quotes it in the same order as does Ya'akov.

In the original Aramaic text of Mark, we have the same reversed order of appearance:

> **Mark 10:19 Etheridge**   Thou knowest the commandments, Thou shalt not commit adultery, Thou shalt not steal, Thou shalt not kill, Thou shalt not witness false testimony, Thou shalt not injure, Honour thy father and thy mother.

In Romans, Rabbi Sha'ul quotes it in the same order as had Yeshua and Ya'akov.

> **Romans 13:9 ESV**   For the commandments, "You shall not commit adultery, You shall not murder, You shall not steal, You shall not covet," and any other commandment, are summed up in this word: "You shall love your neighbor as yourself."

This same order can be found in the Greek translation of the Hebrew scriptures, called the Septuagint, in "Codex B."

> **Deuteronomy 5:17**   And you shall not commit adultery.

Deuteronomy 5:18 You shall not murder.

Certain Hebrew manuscripts, namely that which is called Codex B of chapter five of Deuteronomy, and another ancient manuscript which we still have today called the Nash papyrus (which contains the Decalogue of chapter twenty of Exodus, and the Shema found in the sixth chapter of Deuteronomy) has this same reversed order. Even Philo, the Greek historian, quotes Deuteronomy in this same apparent reversed order. Why?

This reversed order was apparently the order of many, but not all, of the scrolls used during that time period. And therefore, we don't have to guess at which book Ya'akov is quoting. We know! It couldn't be Exodus, because only Deuteronomy has them flipped in this order in some of the scrolls. The reason for this minor discrepancy? We can only speculate. Some believe it was because the crime of adultery was considered even more grievous than murder because adultery is said to murder more than just the soul of the individual by its practice, but whole family structures. Therefore, it is placed before murder in the order of social importance. For whatever reason, this points us back to the preference of Ya'akov in quoting from Deuteronomy instead of Exodus.

We touched on this in the last chapter, but the importance of the book of Deuteronomy (Devarim) cannot be overstated. This book has had a tremendous influence upon Jewish practice. When one thinks of the Jewish worship service, either ancient or modern, we must be moved by the fact that it's in Deuteronomy that one finds the most significant readings. And this importance is reflected in the text of Ya'akov.

The sixth chapter (the Shema passage), is the cornerstone of modern Judaism. The very reason for a public reading of the Torah is founded in chapter thirty-one. The B'rachah (or blessing) after meals comes from chapter eight. The Kiddush on the Sabbath day can be found in chapter five. The placing of the Mezuzah, the wearing of tefillin, the use of the tzitzit – all these are all from the book of Deuteronomy!

Dr. Jeffrey Tigay, professor of Hebrew and Semitic Languages at the University of Pennsylvania, has noted:

> Deuteronomy is the source of the concept that religious life should be based on a sacred book and its study. As the biblical book that deals most explicitly with beliefs and attitudes, it plays a major role in Jewish theology. In the theological- ethical introduction of his digest of Jewish law, the Mishneh Torah, Maimonides cites Deuteronomy more than any other book, starting with the command to believe in God and Him alone... Deuteronomy's effect on Jewish life cannot be overstated. No idea has shaped Jewish history more than monotheism, which this book asserts so passionately.[103]

Can we derive from this that Deuteronomy was the principle part of the Torah scroll used during the childhood of both Ya'akov and Yeshua, and possibly during the formational years of Sha'ul of Tarsus? Absolutely! The place of Deuteronomy within the Jewish community was a very prominent place! The impact of this book on the Jewish child, the Jewish home, the Jewish synagogue, and the Jewish community was, and is still, enormous!

Now, let's pick up where we left off in the last chapter.

v.19 You believe that God is one. You do well! Even the demons believe and tremble.

Not only is the order of the commands from Deuteronomy firmly fixed within the mind of Ya'akov, but so is the Shema, it's central message. *"Hear Israel: Adonai our God, Adonai is one (echad)."*

---

103 Tigay, Dr. Jeffrey From his article entitled "Deuteronomy and Judaism." Dr. Jeffrey Tigay is A.M. Ellis Professor of Hebrew and Semitic Languages and Literatures at the University of Pennsylvania.

Deuteronomy 6:4 ESV   Hear, O Israel: The LORD our God, the LORD is one.

This passage is the bedrock of Judaism. That God is One. He is in unity with Himself. The Hebrew of this passage is pronounced like this:

"Shema Yisrael, Adonai, Elohainu, Adonai echad."

Rabbi Simeon Ben Joachi is quoted as saying:

"Come and see the mystery of the word Elohim. There are three degrees, and each degree is by itself alone, and yet they are all one, and joined together in one, and are not divided from each other."[104]

A primary understanding of the character of God is essential. But, note that an understanding of God, even an understanding of God's plan, is not enough. Ya'akov continues:

> **v.20**   Now do you want to understand, oh frail man, that faith without works is dead?

Let's take a look at the unique qualities of this verse.

The phrase "oh frail man" is an Aramaic phrase based on it's sound.
It would be like us, saying of a person, "Georgie Porgie," or of an animal, "antelope cantaloupe." In Aramaic, it's: "bar-nasha khalasha." It's a rhyme that has rhythm. "O weak man." Our teacher uses this rhyming technique to grab our attention.

And what does he say? That emunah without action is lazy? No! That emunah without action is inactive? No! That emnuah without action is

---

104   The Treasure of Scripture Knowledge: Five Hundred Thousand Scripture References and Parallel Passages, Introduction by R. A. Torrey (Oak Harbor: Logos Research Systems, Inc., 1995), Electronic edition.

idle? No![105] But, this is how some of the Greek translations have come down to us.[106] Unfortunately, it really dumbs down the intent of the Aramaic text. The Aramaic has "to be dead!" or "mat". This takes us back to it's kin Hebrew term of "mot," which reminds us of the bondage in Egypt and of the god of the underworld, or of those who are dead. Quite fitting, don't you think?

So, this rhythmic phrase "Bar-nasha Khalasha" pictures the person without actions as *"frail, feeble, weak, unwarlike, faint-hearted, unfortunate, unlucky."*[107] Then He dies! This is precisely what Ya'akov says happens to a person's faith or "understanding" of God when they neglect to put their faith into motion for God. The real and true faith that is a gift from God simply gets sick and dies!

Rabbi Sha'ul says:

> **Romans 12:3 ESV**   For by the grace given to me I say to everyone among you not to think of himself more highly than he ought to think, but to think with sober judgment, each according to the measure of faith that God has assigned.

If each of us is given a "measure of faith," then each of us is also given the ability we need to live out that "faith" by that same measure of action! It's time for the people of God to become people of action! There's a time for training, to be discipled, to learn, to grow, to reflect, to adjust. Then, there's the time to make sure that we're putting into practice each and every thing that we've learned to do.

---

105   Each of these are examples from Friberg's Analytical Greek Lexicon under the article "argos" including: "inactive, not working, idle, unemployed, and of persons wanting nothing to do lazy"

106   The Wescott and Hort Greek text is a great example of the use of this term "arge" (lazy) which is found in the Alexandrian manuscript family, while the Textus Receptus and the Byzantine manuscripts have "nekra" (to be dead). This is the meaning here in the Aramaic Peshitta text.

107   Payne Smith Syriac Dictionary, pg. 145.

Just as faith is something that is given in measure, there's another element that is given the same way: grace!

Ephesians 4:7 ESV   But grace was given to each one of us according to the measure of Christ's gift.

Faith apart from works isn't *useless* as the English Standard translates it. In reality, it's *dead!* And just in case we didn't hear him clearly, Ya'akov gives us more examples so that we don't misconstrue his meaning. And the first example that he gives is the example of Father Abraham.

> **vs.21-23**   Was not our father Abraham justified by works when he offered Isaac his son on the altar? (22) You see that his faith aided his works and [that] by works, his faith was matured. (23) And the scripture was fulfilled that said: ABRAHAM BELIEVED IN GOD AND IT WAS COUNTED TO HIM FOR JUSTIFICATION, and he was called the friend of God.

The term "justified" here is the same word used for "to be made righteous." The word is "zadak" in Aramaic, and "tzadik" in Hebrew. It means: "*to be declared righteous; approved, acquitted; think it right, or act rightly.*"[108]

Not only that, but it's a perfect tense verb, meaning that it's a completed action and not a work in progress. Now, when Abraham acted upon his understanding of God he was then counted by God as a "righteous person." And this of course happened as a result of the "Akedah" (the Binding), as Abraham followed through with the specific task at hand. That task: to sacrifice his son, Isaac.

---

108 BibleWorks Peshitta Lexicon, "zadak"

103

Chapter 10

This is place where we left off in our last chapter.

> **vs.21-23**   Was not our father Abraham justified by works when he offered Isaac his son on the altar? (22) You see that his faith aided his works and [that] by works, his faith was matured. (23) And the scripture was fulfilled that said: ABRAHAM BELIEVED IN GOD AND IT WAS COUNTED TO HIM FOR JUSTIFICATION, and he was called the friend of God.

Concerning "the binding," Ya'akov employs a seldom used term for the word "offering." It's the word "seleq." And it means: *"to go up, come up, ascend, climb up, enter; rise up, well up, dawn, grow up."*[109]

Seleq is used to describe not only an offering, but an offering made on the top of a hill or a mountain. This is the perfect word to describe the binding of Isaac. It paints a picture of Abraham and his son, climbing to the mountain summit in order to offer to God a fitting sacrifice. It also paints a picture for us of Abraham's faith as "growing up" or "maturing."

When the rabbis discuss "the binding," there is much oral tradition which surrounds this monumental act of faith. Here is one of those stories.

"When Abraham finally held the knife over his beloved son, Isaac seemed doomed, and the angels of heaven shed tears which

---

109 Ibid., "seleq"

fell upon Isaac's eyes, causing him blindness in later life. But their prayer was heard. The Lord sent Michael the archangel to tell Abraham not to sacrifice his son, and the dew of life was poured on Isaac to revive him. The ram to be offered in his place had stood there ready, *prepared from the beginning of Creation.* [110]

I'm fascinated by the thought that the substitute for the offering had been prepared before the beginning ever began! What a picture of what the Messiah has done for us!

Yeshua became our substitute. He took our place. He climbed that exact hill. He bore those nails. He carried our sin. He bore our punishment. Yeshua, as the Lamb that was slain, would use the same language about His death as that used by the rabbis when telling the story of the akedah (the binding). In their story, it was the ram that was preselected before creation. In Yeshua's story, it was He, Himself.

> **John 17:24 ESV** Father, I desire that they also, whom you have given me, may be with me where I am, to see my glory that you have given me because you loved me *before the foundation of the world.*

Regarding Abraham, Ya'akov has told us that "faith aided his works." Literally, that means that his trust in God "relieved" his actions. What Abraham, as a father, was asked to do was beyond what any loving parent could possibly accomplish. But, because he trusted the character of God, he did it anyway.

Ya"akov finishes his sentence with:

> **v.22b** ...and [that] by works, his faith was matured.

The Aramaic term that Ya'akov uses here for "complete" is: "gemar" and

---

110 M. Avoth v.6

it means: "*to be perfect, mature; to accomplish, complete, fulfill; to perform, bring to an end, finish, spend, or use up.*"[111] It wasn't until Abraham actually put his faith in action that it became mature. His *works* or *actions* made his faith in God complete. So, what is it that God has been asking you to do? My strong suggestion is that you do it, so that you may begin to function on a more mature level in your relationship with God. It's good advice. Ya'akov would agree! Maybe this is why the church today is such an immature body, meandering about with little purpose, with believers who merely understand faith in their thoughts, but don't act upon it. This is like the phenomenon we have in the west with school girls who are babies themselves, having babies. No wonder Christianity has become primarily a system of belief, not a system of change.

> **v.23** And the scripture was fulfilled that said: ABRAHAM BELIEVED IN GOD AND IT WAS COUNTED TO HIM FOR JUSTIFICATION, and he was called the friend of God.

I love the phrase "the friend of God (Elohim)." That is definitely something that I would want to be said of me. One of the traditional background stories regarding this event is found in the apocryphal Book of Jubilees, where it says:

> "For he was found faithful (believing), and was written down upon the heavenly tablets as the friend of God."[112]

It's in the Jewish work entitled, The Wisdom of Solomon, that we find that the term "friends of God" used as an expression for the "righteous".[113]

Back to our text. Did you notice what Ya'akov is doing here? He's

---

111 NT Peshitta Morphology, Notes and Lexicon - Janet Magiera
112 Jubilees, 19.9
113 Wisdom 7.27

combining two completely separate historical events together into one cohesive story with a beginning and an end.

In the twenty-first verse, Ya'akov takes us to the events of Genesis twenty-two and the story of the akedah.

> **Genesis 22:1-6 ESV**   After these things God tested Abraham and said to him, "Abraham!" And he said, "Here I am." (2) He said, "Take your son, your only son Isaac, whom you love, and go to the land of Moriah, and offer him there as a burnt offering on one of the mountains of which I shall tell you." (3) So Abraham rose early in the morning, saddled his donkey, and took two of his young men with him, and his son Isaac. And he cut the wood for the burnt offering and arose and went to the place of which God had told him. (4) On the third day Abraham lifted up his eyes and saw the place from afar. (5) Then Abraham said to his young men, "Stay here with the donkey; I and the boy will go over there and worship and come again to you." (6) And Abraham took the wood of the burnt offering and laid it on Isaac his son. And he took in his hand the fire and the knife. So they went both of them together...

The story continues as Abraham is just about to drive the dagger into his son's heart – and the ram appears to take Isaac's place.

I'd like to point out that Isaac is mature enough to carry the wood from the servants on his own back. Rabbinical tradition says that he"s probably in his thirties by this point. *(This, of course, matches the age of Yeshua as He carried His wood, a Roman cross, up the very same hill to be our sacrifice.)*

But, here's Ya'akov's point: It was decades between "the binding" of Isaac, and the time when God called Abram righteous. Just when was it that God gave him that designation?

> **Genesis 15:5-6 ESV**   And he brought him outside and said,

"Look toward heaven, and number the stars, if you are able to number them." Then he said to him, "So shall your offspring be." (6) And he believed the LORD, and he counted it to him as righteousness.

Abram, back before Isaac was even conceived, completely believed God to be permanently faithful.[114]

Ya'akov quotes from Genesis, where God was then "forecasting" him to be righteous. That is, in essence, what this Hebrew verb "chashab" depicts – a forecast. Whereas Abram's "believing" was the conclusion of his estimation of God's character, God's estimation of Abram's faith was anything but finished. It was in-process, mostly because Abram's will and future actions played a significant role. This is indicated by the use of an imperfect verb here.[115] God's "forecasting"[116] of Abram's faith would become a completed action when Abraham took the final step in actualizing his faith. He trusted, but it was only later that he finally acted upon his faith. It wasn't until the action of the akedah that he actually becomes righteous. Before then, Abram was only "considered" as righteous. Because faith without action cannot become mature. Or, as Ya'akov puts it:

James 2:22b ESV "...by the works his faith was rendered complete."

Rabbi Sha'ul wrote to the believers in Ephesus about this same principle of faith and works:

Ephesians 2:8-9 ESV For by grace you have been saved

---

114 "To Believe" here is the Hebrew term "aman" and it's in the Hiphil stem, and is in the perfect tense. It indicates a completed estimation of a person or situation. i.e. Abram considered God to be completely trustworthy.

115 "Counted" here is the Hebrew "chashab" it is used here in the Qal/Imperfect form.

116 See Strongs #2803 where "chashab" can be translated, "to weave, to fabricate, to plot, to think, regard, value, compute, to consider, count, devise, esteem, forecast, imagine, etc."

through faith. And this is not your own doing; it is the gift of God, (9) not a result of works, so that no one may boast.

Notice that the good Rabbi doesn't stop there. He completes his statement in the next verse by affirming that true faith leads to action.

Ephesians 2:10 ESV For we are his workmanship, created in Christ Jesus for good works, which God prepared beforehand, that we should walk in them.

Sha'ul and Ya'akov are definitely on the same page.

I think that it's pretty cool that God "forecasted" Abram's follow-thru and therefore also his righteousness. Another way of translating that God "counted" him as being righteous is with the word "imagined." God imagined Abram as acting on His word, therefore He saw him as the end result: righteous.

> **v. 24** You see that by works a man is justified and not by faith alone.

Over thirty years passed between the time of God's initial declaration of Abram, and Abraham's action. Yet, God was able to see the end from the beginning of Abram's faith. How does God see you? What is the end result that God sees when He initially imagined your life, your faith, your walk, or your actions? If you'd like a sneak preview of what God saw when He first imagined you, just start walking it out and it will become clearer. You become what you live. Your big steps equal the sum of your small steps. Therefore, we should all live right now in the manner that we want to end up. We always end up down the road that we travel on today. If you're not traveling anywhere, then get up! Your decisions today will be the primary contributors to what your spiritual life looks like tomorrow.

It was Abram's faith in God that led to His follow-thru in offering up

Isaac, which led to the maturing of His faith, which God forecasted would take place decades in advance. Every decision and action that you make affects your maturity and ultimately your destiny! Do you consider God to be perfectly faithful? Are you living with that fundamental premise in view? Abram did, and it was credited to him as righteousness. That's the reason that Ya'akov uses him as an example of biblical faith.

To conclude, Ya'akov gives us one final example:

> **v.25**   So also, was not Rahab the harlot justified by works when she took in the spies and sent them out by another way?

By mentioning Rahab directly after mentioning father Abraham, it speaks volumes about the significance of Rahab in Jewish thinking, and also about the significance of gentiles in the heart of Ya'akov. Ya'akov's examples both speak of gentiles responding by faith. Both Abraham and Rahab were born outside of the influence of the Hebrews, yet both responded to God and became shining examples among the Hebrews/Jews of what true faith in God truly is. I find it interesting that Ya'akov would choose as his examples one person raised in idolatry (Abram) and another raised in harlotry (Rahab). Each were the products of the land that needed to be reformed and reclaimed by God.

That is such a great example of what God can do in us when we're willing to say yes.

In the ancient work entitled, The Testament of the Twelve Patriarchs, we read:

"But the spirit of love works together with the law of God."[117]

---

117 Testament of the Twelve Patriarchs, Gad. iv. 7.

This is the gist of it. Both Abraham and Rahab acted-upon and acted-out their faith. Their understanding of God demanded that their lives changed as a result. And because of their acted-out faith, God considered them to be "just," tzadik, RIGHT!

So, when we just have a philosophy about God, but don't prove that philosophy by living it out in the real world, are we then considered to be wrong? Think about it!

Ya'akov finishes chapter two with this statement:

> **James 2:26 MGI**   As the body without the spirit is dead, so also faith without works is dead.

The phrase "the body without the spirit" was a common Jewish idiom of the day.[118] Ya'akov is saying that in the same way a dead body is unclean, a person's belief system, without action, is unclean. No one should come into contact with either one of these. A person who had come into contact with a dead body could not come near to God, until the proper ritual cleansing was performed. According to the nineteenth chapter of the book of Numbers, there were "actions" that needed to be taken before this person's unclean status would change.

In the same way, before coming near to God, a person with an unclean faith must change his status as well. He must be considered clean again, and given our context, this means he must get up and put his faith into action, and be considered alive again!

By the way, do you remember what the key mechanisms were which made the person clean and once again able to approach God?

Numbers 19:17 ESV   For the unclean they shall take some

---

118   Ohel. Moed, fol. 15.1

ashes of the burnt sin offering, and fresh water shall be added in a vessel.

Fresh water was used throughout this process of cleansing – not *stagnant* water, but running, *fresh* water. Actually, the Hebrew term is "mayim chayim," which means: "*living water.*"

This is a picture of what the Messiah has done for us. We were dead in our sins and trespasses. We were literally, in the spiritual sense, walking corpses. Were, that is, until the Messiah brought us His "Mayim Chayim." His blood, like living water, has made us ceremonially cleansed and acceptable before God. We have been given a second chance to live, and in faith, we are indebted through love to act upon that which has been entrusted to us.

Remember the account of Yeshua talking to the woman at the well? This woman had an ongoing sin problem. What was it that the Master said to her? *"Come drink living water."*

> **John 4:10-14 ESV**   Jesus answered her, "If you knew the gift of God, and who it is that is saying to you, 'Give me a drink,' you would have asked him, and he would have given you living water (mayim chayim)." (11) The woman said to him, "Sir, you have nothing to draw water with, and the well is deep. Where do you get that living water (mayim chayim)? (12) Are you greater than our father Jacob? He gave us the well and drank from it himself, as did his sons and his livestock." (13) Jesus said to her, "Everyone who drinks of this water will be thirsty again, (14) but whoever drinks of the water that I will give him will never be thirsty again. The water that I will give him will become in him a spring of water welling up to eternal life."

Here's another example of Yeshua referring to himself as mayim chayim:

> **John 7:37-38 ESV**   On the last day of the feast, the great day,

Jesus stood up and cried out, "If anyone thirsts, let him come to me and drink. (38) Whoever believes in me, as the Scripture has said, 'Out of his heart will flow rivers of living water (mayim chayim).'"

And at the conclusion of all things we read;

Revelation 7:15-17 ESV "Therefore they are before the throne of God, and serve him day and night in his temple; and he who sits on the throne will shelter them with his presence. (16) They shall hunger no more, neither thirst anymore; the sun shall not strike them, nor any scorching heat. (17) For the Lamb in the midst of the throne will be their shepherd, and he will guide them to springs of living water (mayim chayim), and God will wipe away every tear from their eyes."

Halleluiah! Thanks be to God, who offers us to drink from the cool, life-giving water that flows from the Messiah!

Chapter 11

In our last chapter, we were challenged with the biblical model of faith. Biblical faith is action, and without action faith is dead. Dead faith causes us to be separated from God, as a person who has become ritually unclean

In this chapter, we pick up where we left off in the text. Our next topic: the tongue.

It's important for you to understand the "segway" between the topic of faith and the topic of the tongue. Ya'akov is addressing how we are to communicate. Remember back in the first chapter, Ya'akov addressed the issue of communication during trials.

> **James 1:12 ESV**   Blessed is the man who remains steadfast under trial, for when he has stood the test he will receive the crown of life, which God has promised to those who love him.

And remember that the term translated here "to remain steadfast" also meant: *"to preach and to declare."*

Ya'akov then drove his point home again in the next verse:

> **James 1:13 ESV**   Let no one *say* when he is tempted, "I am being tempted by God," for God cannot be tempted with evil, and he himself tempts no one.

Then, in chapter two, Ya'akov demonstrated to us what appropriate or inappropriate judgment toward others looks like:

James 2:12-14 ESV   So *speak* and so act as those who are to be judged under the law of liberty. (13) For judgment is without mercy to one who has shown no mercy. Mercy triumphs over judgment. (14) What good is it, my brothers, if someone *says* he has faith but does not have works? Can that faith save him?

Ya'akov has been building from the element of our conversations through our trials, to the element of our conversations through our prejudices. Now, this leads to the primary way our speech affects others, or should affect others: through teaching about God.

James 3:1 MGI   You should not have many teachers among you, my brothers, but know that we are liable [to have] a greater judgment.

First, let me give you some examples of this same principle in ancient Judaism, then we'll talk about the position of the teacher.

The Pirke Avot says:

Love labor, and hate the rabbin's office.[119]

In other words, resist becoming a rabbi because the responsibility is great. A rabbi is a teacher of God's instructions. This is what Ya'akov is talking about here.

Yeshua taught about the tremendous sense of responsibility a person has when God entrusts him with something.

Luke 12:47-48 ESV   And that servant who knew his master's will but did not get ready or act according to his will, will receive a severe beating. (48) But the one who did not know, and did what deserved a beating, will receive a light beating.

---

119   Pirke Avot, c.i.10

Everyone to whom much was given, of him much will be required, and from him to whom they entrusted much, they will demand the more.

Again, regarding the topic of being a teacher, hear what Rabbi Natan has to say:

Teachers, a slight error will be compounded by students, who in turn will teach nonsense that will lead their students to seek foreign values.[120]

This is precisely what has been taking place throughout most of church history! By the later half of the first century, teachers began rising up from among the gentiles. These men were those who had either ignorantly or purposely shrugged-off the "Jewishness" of the scriptures. At this point in church history, so-called "theologians" called the Jews "Christ-killers," when in fact, it was my sin and yours that put Him on the cross. This attitude distorted the intended message of the Jewish writers of the New Testament. As a natural result, respect for the Jewish leaders in predominantly gentile congregations began to diminish. We can see the start of this taking place even as early as the time of the Apostles. Here's an example:

3 John 1:9-10 ESV   I have written something to the church, but Diotrephes, who likes to put himself first, *does not acknowledge our authority.* (10) So if I come, I will bring up what he is doing, *talking wicked nonsense against us.* And not content with that, *he refuses to welcome the brothers,* and also stops those who want to and puts them out of the church.

Concerning this type of attitude, the writer of the book of Hebrews says:

Hebrews 13:17 ESV   Obey your leaders and submit to them, for they are keeping watch over your souls, as those who will

---

120   Avot de R. Natan A..11

have to give an account. Let them do this with joy and not with groaning, for that would be of no advantage to you.

The Aramaic text, here, is very direct:

> **Hebrews 13:17 MGI**   Be convicted by your leaders and obey them, for they watch for your lives as men who give an accounting of you, so that with joy they may do this and not with groanings, because that is not profitable for you.[121]

The term for "be convicted" is "pis" which is an imperative verb (a command) and it means: "*to be persuaded, convinced, urged, convicted, to obey*."[122] The term translated "obey" is the Aramaic word "shema," and it too is another imperative verb. It   means: "*to hear, obey, listen, understand, etc.*"[123]

So, believers in congregations are commanded to listen and obey the congregational leader, allowing him to bring needed conviction, which, in turn, brings repentance and has as it's end: salvation and fellowship with God.

Ya'akov says that being a "malpana" (the Aramaic term for teacher) has a "dina yatira," or a "judgment" that is "extraordinary" or "much greater" than ordinary responsibility.[124]

For this reason, one should use wisdom while considering taking the position of a teacher. Which leads on to the warnings regarding the proper usage of the tongue.

---

121   MGI NT Peshitta Translation © 2006 Janet Magiera

122   Magiera, Janet, Peshitta Lexicon entry: ܦܝܣ

123   Ibid., ܫܡܥ

124   See Peshitta Lexicon entry: ܕܝܢܐ

> **James 3:2 MGI** For we all offend [in] many [things]. Anyone who does not offend in word, this [one] is a mature man who is also able to subject his whole body.

Here, Ya'akov includes himself in the weakness of the human condition.[125] He wants his friends to know that he also "offends" at times. The word for "offend" here is "shera" which means: "*to slip, stumble, offend, transgress or to falter.*"[126]

In rabbinical writings, it is common to see texts which counsel against the use of many words, fruitless words, or contradictory words. For example, we find the following advice in the apocryphal book of Sirach:

> **Sirach 5:11-15 NAB-A** Be swift to hear, but slow to answer. (12) If you have the knowledge, answer your neighbor; if not, put your hand over your mouth. (13) Honor and dishonor through talking! A man's tongue can be his downfall. (14) Be not called a detractor; use not your tongue for calumny; For shame has been created for the thief, and the reproach of his neighbor for the double-tongued. (15) Say nothing harmful, small or great;[127]

And again:

> **Sirach 28:12 NAB-A** If you blow upon a spark, it quickens into flame, if you spit on it, it dies out; yet both you do with your mouth![128]

In fact, the rest of this chapter in Sirach (which was written sometime during the second century B.C.E.) contains strong advice and

---

125 Ya'akov uses the 1ˢᵗ person plural form here.

126 Ibid., ܡܫܬܪܝܢ

127 The New American Bible w/ Apocrypha Copyright © 1987 by Confraternity of Christian Doctrine, Inc., Washington, DC.

128 Ibid.

118

admonitions regarding the use of the tongue. The influence that this writing had upon Ya'akov, Sha'ul, and later Judaism, is obvious.

The word Ya'akov uses to describe the man who controls his tongue is, "gevra," which instead of being one who is "perfect" more aptly describes one who is "mighty!"[129] This is in line with it's Hebrew relative, "gevar," which is usually translated as *an upright man, blameless man, or mighty man.* Literally, *"a man of no shame."*[130]

It's this designation that describes the mighty person who can keep control over his little tongue. He appears strong and, through his self control, has nothing to be ashamed over. Notice the purposeful contrast for comedic impact given here between the "mighty man" and the "little tongue."[131] I guess you could say that Ya'akov was saying this with "tongue in cheek." (Ugh!)

This "mighty man" accomplishes the task of subjecting his tongue to his will. Actually though, Ya'akov doesn't say that it's a done deal, like it's a single act accomplished by a mere decision. It's presented here as being an ongoing effort.[132] I'm certainly glad that Ya'akov admits that this herculean task requires a lifetime of herculean effort, because it surely feels that way to me.

The taming of the tongue is tantamount to the taming of an ever illusive monster. How can something so small have such a huge control over our lives? This is not just an enigma that I personally struggle to answer, but one that has been universally pondered throughout human history.

---

129 Ibid., 𐤀𐤁𐤂 "gevra" properly means "man, husband or mighty one"

130 The Complete Word Study Dictionary, H1399 © 1992 By AMG International, Inc. Chattanooga, TN 37422, U.S.A. Revised edition, 1993

131 It's this contrast that leads me to believe that "mighty" is a better translation here than is "perfect" though both are acceptable.

132 The Aramaic verb translated as "to keep" is imperfect, meaning an ongoing, unfinished action. The imperfect tense here may also indicate action without reference of time.

The puzzle then is: how to know what to say, and when and where to say it, and to whom?

As the wise sages have said:

> Better to be silent and thought a fool, than to open one's mouth and remove all doubt!

Now, Ya'akov offers us a couple of examples of the power of our words.

> **James 3:3 MGI** For behold, we place bits in the mouths of horses, so that they may be tamed by us and we turn their whole body.

The horse was known as a strong and fast animal, yet they are easily guided and steered by their mouths.

> **James 3:4 MGI** Also, the mighty boats, although harsh winds drive them, are turned by a small piece of wood to the place that the pilot wants to see.

Ya'akov shows how a huge powerful ship being driven by strong winds can be turned with a tiny rudder. I love the contrasts that are painted for us here. And I love the analogy that the pilot is able to steer his huge vessel by a tiny piece of wood. In which direction is your life heading? Open your mouth and you'll find out by your words.

Here are a couple example from Yeshua regarding the use of the tongue:

> **Matthew 12:34-37 ESV** You brood of vipers! How can you speak good, when you are evil? For out of the abundance of the heart the mouth speaks. (35) The good person out of his good treasure brings forth good, and the evil person out of his evil treasure brings forth evil. (36) I tell you, on the day of judgment

people will give account for every careless word they speak, (37) for by your words you will be justified, and by your words you will be condemned.

Matthew 15:11,18 ESV   It is not what goes into the mouth that defiles a person, but what comes out of the mouth; this defiles a person... (18) But what comes out of the mouth proceeds from the heart, and this defiles a person.

Take a fresh look at Yeshua's words here in Luke:

Luke 6:45-46 ESV   The good person out of the good treasure of his heart produces good, and the evil person out of his evil treasure produces evil, for out of the abundance of the heart his mouth speaks. (46) Why do you call me 'Lord, Lord,' and not do what I tell you?

Yeshua is telling us that a person's words reveal their heart. This is why He finishes the statement with the question: *"Why do you call me 'Lord, Lord,' and not do what I tell you?"* Whenever there's a contradiction between the words being said and the actions being done, the person must be considered evil or twisted. When the mouth and the actions do not line-up, that's a sign of being broken and in a sinful state. Yeshua says here, *Why would you consider me Marah[133], yet refuse to obey me?* The answer is very clear. This person obviously doesn't fear God or is wavering in his belief that Yeshua is God, or at the very least, one who has the authority of God.

Our Master had quite a lot to say about the words that we speak, and the impact He had on Ya'akov is apparent in his letter.

Ya'akov now continues with this topic by listing some of the negative consequences of not bridling our tongues. The following are a couple of verses which have been mistranslated due to adaptations in our Greek

---

133   Here the Aramaic text has Marah, which can be translated as Lord and is often used to designate Almighty God.

text. I'll give you the typical translation from the Greek first, then we'll compare that to the original Aramaic.

> **James 3:5-6 ESV** So also the tongue is a small member, yet it boasts of great things. How great a forest is set ablaze by such a small fire! (6) And the tongue is a fire, a world of unrighteousness. The tongue is set among our members, staining the whole body, setting on fire the entire course of life, and set on fire by hell.

This demonstrates the tongues' negative affect upon a person's life. That's fairly intense, however, the Aramaic text is much more graphic.

> **James 3:5-6 MGI**   So also, the tongue is a small member and it elevates itself. Also, a small fire causes large forests to burn. (6) And the tongue is a fire and the world of sin is like a forest. And the tongue, although it is [one] among the members, marks our whole body and sets on fire the successions of our generations that roll on as wheels and it also burns with fire.

The Aramaic text shows that the negative affect of our words not only affect our own lives, but they affect the lives of generations to come!

How many of us have been affected by the insensitive words of struggling parents? And how long do these type of hurtful words stay with a child? That type of wound usually stays with the person throughout their entire life. And, if not dealt with, these very words are then passed on to another generation, and another and another. This cycle will continue unless, and until, that destructive chain is broken and control of the tongue is mastered. Here is what the midrash has on the portion of Leviticus called "Metzora:"

"The tongue...exploits, the tongue wreaks havoc. It is worse

122

than the worst of sins."[134]

There's even a tradition among the sages that recalls the original sin. It speculates as to why humans have a line down the center of their tongues. Their explanation is that God placed a line down the center of man's tongue as a reminder to every generation not to lie about our sins. If true, that means we each carry a reminder that when we lie, *we are like the deceiving snake with the forked tongue.*

134 See, Midrash Tanh. Lev., "Metzora" 4-5

Chapter 12

We have learned from our study in the last chapter that the words we say can affect many generations in the future. Ya'akov now invokes another illustration – this one from nature.

> **James 3:7 MGI**   For all the natures of animals and of birds and reptiles, of the sea and of dry land, are subjected to the nature of mankind.

Here, the term for nature is "keyana," meaning: *"twice."* Keyana is: *"that which comes from the natural disposition, or in the order of that produced by sexual intercourse, or that which is produced by the species naturally."*[135]

The same four categories listed by Ya'akov are delineated for us in the book of Genesis and in 1 Kings. We read here concerning man's dominion over the animal kingdom:

> **Genesis 9:2 ESV**   The fear of you and the dread of you shall be upon every beast of the earth and upon every bird of the heavens, upon everything that creeps on the ground and all the fish of the sea. Into your hand they are delivered.

> **1 Kings 4:33 ESV**   He spoke of trees, from the cedar that is in Lebanon to the hyssop that grows out of the wall. He spoke also of beasts, and of birds, and of reptiles, and of fish.

These are not the only examples of these four categories being used in

---

135   See Magiera's Dictionary No.1154 under ܟܝܢܐ

scripture. Genesis has had a profound affect upon all the scriptures which came afterwards, and therefore upon Judaism as a whole. Interestingly, the Greek text of James contains neither occurrence of the term "nature" that's found in the Aramaic text, yet it's this very topic of "nature" that's being highlighted by Ya'akov in verse seven.

In the text of Genesis, man is seen as having the animal kingdom placed under his care. Ya'akov says that the animal world has been placed in the position of a servant, an "evad," which means one who is *submissive, tamed" and even seen as being "enslaved,"*[136] in this case, to humanity.

Rabbi Sha'ul writes concerning this subjection:

> **Romans 8:20-21 ESV** For the creation was subjected to futility, not willingly, but because of him who subjected it, in hope (21) that the creation itself will be set free from its bondage to corruption and obtain the freedom of the glory of the children of God.

Then, Ya'akov goes on to say:

> **James 3:8 MGI** But the tongue, no one is able to subdue. This evil, when it is not restrained, is full of the poison of death.

The tongue wasn't mentioned in the four categories of life which are naturally subjected to man. For man to subject the tongue under his control, it's going to take a lot of extra effort on his part!

Adam Clarke makes the following observation about the imagery here:

> "He (Ya'akov) refers here to the tongues of serpents, supposed to be the means of conveying their poison into wounds made by

---

136 Ibid., #1724

their teeth."[137]

It seems that the original sin, instigated by the serpent back in the garden, continues to plague mankind by means of the tongue. If you will recall, it was through the deception of the serpent's tongue that God was misrepresented, causing mankind to fall. The tongue has continued throughout time to be the chief instrument of man's demise. It must be restrained because it is full of the serpent's venom!

In Judaism, the sin of "lashon hara'" is considered to be one of the most despicable sins one can commit. It is literally, *"the tongue of the evil"* and it's what we typically define as being *"gossip, backbiting, slander."*[138] Is it any wonder then that the rabbis would point to the line down the middle of humanity's tongue as a reminder of our having sided with the lying serpent in the garden?

I believe the Psalmist has this very thing in mind when he writes:

> **Psalms 140:3 ESV**   They make their tongue sharp as a serpent's, and under their lips is the venom of asps. Selah.

In the Talmud, there's an interesting section on the use of the tongue. Here's a portion of it:

> The Holy One, blessed be He, said to the tongue: All members of the human body are standing, you are lying; all members of the human body are outside, you are guarded inside; not only that, but I surrounded you with two walls, one of bone and one of flesh; 'What shall be given unto thee, what shall be done more unto thee, thou deceitful tongue'! And R. Johanan said in the name of R. Joseph b. Zimra: One who bears evil tales almost denies the foundation [of faith]. as it is said: Who have said:

---

137 Adam Clarke's Commentary on the Bible, James 3:8
138 Stern, Jewish New Testament Commentary - James 3:8

Our tongue will we make mighty; our lips are with us; who is lord over us?[139]

It's in this same section we find this obvious connection to our study:

> R. Hama b. Hanina said: What is the remedy for slanderers? If he be a scholar, let him engage in the Torah, as it is said: The healing for a tongue is the tree of life, and 'tongue' here means the evil tongue, as it is said: 'Their tongue is a sharpened arrow', and 'tree [of life]' means only the Torah, as it is said: She is a tree of life, to them that lay hold upon her.[140]

Once again, concerning the sin of the tongue, we're forced back to its origin in the garden, and to it's cure: the tree of life. It is no coincidence that the Torah itself is attached to wooden posts which are called "trees of life."

As there were two trees in the Garden, one which gave life and one, death, so Ya'akov points out the two usages of the tongue.

> **James 3:9-10 MGI**   With it we bless the LORD and Father and with it we curse men, who are made in the likeness of God. (10) And from the same mouth proceed blessings and cursings. My brothers, it is not right that these [things] be done so.

Once again, Ya'akov takes us right back to the earliest beginnings of man as recorded in the first book of Moshe, Breishit (Genesis). Here, he points to the source of blessings and the source of curses and compares this to the affect of our speech. He has been focusing our attention on the very beginning, as if to say, *"This is anything but a new problem."* Often times when a coach recognizes a developing problem within an athlete or a team, he will take them back through the basics in order to

---

139   Babylonian Talmud, Mas. Arachin 15b (Soncino Edition)
140   Ibid.

help them correct the offending habit. The question that we need to start asking ourselves is, what is the offending habit that Ya'akov is addressing?

If we were going to successfully "break down" this text, we do well to look first at the Genesis account from which Ya'akov is quoting. It's there we see that man was made in the "likeness" of God.

> **Genesis 1:26 ESV**   Then God said, "Let us make man in our image, after our likeness. And let them have dominion over the fish of the sea and over the birds of the heavens and over the livestock and over all the earth and over every creeping thing that creeps on the earth."

It is highly plausible, as Ariel Fruchtenbaum notes, the phrase Ya'akov uses in verse nine, that with the tongue we *"bless the Lord and Father"* probably refers to the Jewish tradition of saying, "Blessed be He" after every mention of God's Name. The blessing of God, of course, is absolutely the highest use of the tongue.[141] This is set in contrast to the "cursing of men" who are made in His image.

The word that Ya'akov uses for "to be made" is the Aramaic word "evad." This is interesting because it's the very same word he used in verse seven to convey man's dominion over the animal kingdom. In doing this, Ya'akov is making a specific point. Let's try not to miss it.

Ya'akov is saying that God placed the animals under man, and man under Him! The animals are "subjected to the nature of man," whereas man is "subjected to God's likeness." So, Ya'akov is contrasting the "nature" of man with the "likeness" of God by using this same word for "to subject" in both verses.

What's the difference between the nature of something and the likeness of something?

---

141   Fruchtenbaum, Ariel's Bible Commentary (The Jewish Epistles), pg. 281

Well, the nature (keyana) of something, if you recall, indicates it's *"natural disposition."*[142] But, the likeness (demutha) of something indicates it's *"manner, type or pattern."*[143] The former focuses on the physical, natural or reproductive, while the latter is focused on the spiritual, ethical or behavioral (one's conscience).

Having been created in it, we are subjected to the "likeness" or "image" of God.

> **Genesis 1:27-28 ESV** So God created man in his own *image*, in the *image* of God he created him; male and female he created them. (28) And God blessed them. And God said to them, "Be fruitful and multiply and fill the earth and subdue it, and have dominion over the fish of the sea and over the birds of the heavens and over every living thing that moves on the earth."

It's also important to note that the word for "subjecting" the tongue in verse eight is not the same word used for the subjecting of animals in verse seven, or for the subjecting of man under God as seen in verse nine.

This is an entirely different word that is found in the very same portion of Genesis that Ya'akov's been pointing us towards. It's the word that is used for the concept of man "subduing" the earth (by the way, this Genesis comparison only works in the original language of Aramaic).

> **Genesis 1:28 ESV** "...be fruitful and multiply and fill the earth and subdue it..."

The Hebrew term is "kabash." In Aramaic, it's pronounced "kevash." These terms both mean: *"to bring into bondage, make subservient."*[144]

---

142 Magiera, Ibid., no. 1154

143 Ibid., no.0542 Note: I have purposely only used this terms definitions which describe the nature or substance in lieu of the physical aspect of this word, seeing that Elohim is described as having never been seen by man.

144 Brown, Driver, Briggs, " כבש " H3533

So, Ya'akov is being humorous here. He's saying that man is capable of subduing the whole world, but he's not capable of subduing his own tongue!

> **James 3:11 MGI** Can sweet and bitter water come out of one fountain?

Sixth-century historian, St. Isidorus, wrote about a community of people living in Ethiopia with a lake that would produce bitter water three times each day and then sweet water three times each day, but never at the same time.[145] Is it possible that Ya'akov was aware of this lake? What makes this highly possible is the fact that Ethiopian Jews came up to Jerusalem every year for the feasts. It's a fun thought, but let's get back to the point Ya'akov is trying to make. To have both blessings and curses coming from the same source is unnatural, unlikely, and impossible!

> **James 3:12 MGI** Or can a fig tree, my brothers, produce olives, or a vine, figs? So also, you cannot make salty water sweet.

These statements were well-known proverbs of the day. Here's another one of many which is found in the Talmud:

"Every pumpkin can be told from its stalk."[146]

Yeshua used this same type of proverb in His Sermon on the Mount:

> **Matthew 7:16-20 ESV** You will recognize them by their fruits. Are grapes gathered from thorn bushes, or figs from thistles? (17) So, every healthy tree bears good fruit, but the diseased tree

---

145   See Isidore of Seville's Etymologies: Complete English Translation, Volume 2, XIII, 14.1

146   Babylonian Talmud, Berachot 48a (Soncino Edition)

bears bad fruit. (18) A healthy tree cannot bear bad fruit, nor can a diseased tree bear good fruit. (19) Every tree that does not bear good fruit is cut down and thrown into the fire. (20) Thus you will recognize them by their fruits.

The point is obvious. What comes out of a person is what lies buried within him. Or, who a person is can be seen by how a person lives.

Chapter 13

If you recall, Ya'akov has been discussing how we should speak to one another. He then gave several examples of the tremendous effort it takes to bring our tongues into submission to our will. He took us all the way back to the garden and the first destructive example of the improper use of the tongue. In this section, he's about to make his main point, and he offers it in the form of a question:

> **James 3:13 MGI** Who is wise and instructed among you? He should show his works with praiseworthy actions, with humble wisdom.

The term used here for being *wise* takes us all the way back to chapter one:

> **James 1:5 ESV** If any of you lacks wisdom, let him ask God, who gives generously to all without reproach, and it will be given him.

Remember, the Aramaic term for "wisdom" is "khekmat" and it means: "*to be wise, clever, cunning, shrewd.*" This passive participle carries the added meaning: "*learned and intelligent.*"[147]

Well, Ya'akov is referring not only to one who is "wise" but one who is "*instructed.*" The word for "instructed" is the Aramaic term "reda" which means: "*to journey, travel, proceed; to instruct, chastise, punish, discipline,*

---

147 Magiera, ܚܟܝܡܐ Dictionary No. 0790

correct, train, guide; to follow, and to continue in."[148] It's in the passive voice here, meaning that the person to which Ya'akov is referring has received training. He has been instructed, corrected and has been forced to study. For this reason, he is able to instruct others. Ya'akov is, of course, referring to the rabbi or congregational leader.

As a means of substantiating this, when the Aramaic was translated into the common language of Greek, the translators chose the term "epistemon" to convey this very idea. The "epistemon" was not only considered a learned person but was considered to be an *"expert."*[149]
This word is translated in some versions as: *understanding or knowledge, yet is defined by some as, "to know thoroughly, understand. Endued with knowledge, understanding, expertise, the equivalent to the English "scientist."*[150]

So, let's put some pieces together here. In the day and age when the local synagogue and leader was the primary (if not the only) source to the scriptures, Ya'akov was almost certainly referring here to the congregational teachers. Ya'akov is definitely still on the subject of the tongue, but is now including within it, teaching.

We would be wise to remind ourselves of the importance that the subject of wisdom played in the early Jewish writings. Here's just one example:

> There are seven things that are characteristic in a man of imperfectly developed mind, and seven in a wise man: A wise man speaks not before one who is greater than he in wisdom, and enters not into the midst of the words of his fellow; And is not hasty to answer; He asks in accordance with the subject-matter, and he answers in accordance with the accepted decision; And he speaks of the first point first, and of the last point last;

---

148 Ibid., ܪܒܝ Dictionary No: 2299

149 Gingrich, ἐπιστήμων pg, 76

150 The Complete Word Study Dictionary © 1992 By AMG International, Inc. Chattanooga, TN 37422, U.S.A. Revised edition, 1993

And concerning that which he has not heard, he says: Have not heard; and he acknowledges the truth. And the reverse of these are characteristics in a man of imperfectly developed mind.[151]

Shlomo (Solomon), the wise king, told us:

> **Ecclesiastes 8:1 ESV** Who is like the wise? And who knows the interpretation of a thing? A man's wisdom makes his face shine, and the hardness of his face is changed.

Rabbi Sha'ul (Paul) remarked:

> **1 Corinthians 6:5 ESV** I say this to your shame. Can it be that there is no one among you wise enough to settle a dispute between the brothers...

Here, the rabbi is certainly referring to those who functioned as the "Beit Din" in the local congregational setting. The congregation at Corinth was one primarily made up of gentiles. With this in mind, how important are Rabbi Sha'ul's instructions for us in gentile congregations today? Extremely! A congregation must have wise and godly men and women in places of leadership to have the desperately needed wisdom and balance of an assembly. It's not wise to place young and inexperienced congregational leaders over congregations unless there is some form of Beit Din who can help guide and further disciple them.

This is certainly the exact situation Ya'akov is addressing in his letter as he poses this question:

v.13a Who is wise and instructed among you?

Contrast "wisdom," which is pictured as a humble, ever-working servant, to the Greek "sophia," whose speech just sounds wise.

---

151 Babylonian Talmud, Mishna – Mas. Avoth 5.7 (Soncino Edition)

Kittle gives this as part of the description of "sophia:"

> "Sophia is derived from an adjective and always denotes a quality, never an activity."[152]

Wow, it's just as I've been saying. The Greek mindset was definitely not the Jewish mindset. To the Jew, wisdom meant doing something. To the Greek, merely formulating a wise conclusion was enough.

Ya'akov says the wisdom which is so desperately needed must be "*meek or humble.*"[153]

v.13b ...with *humble* wisdom.

Another way to translate "humble" might be "*modest.*" This reminds us of the words of the Messiah, who calls us to follow His example of meekness.

> **Matthew 11:28-30 ESV**   Come to me, all who labor and are heavy laden, and I will give you rest. (29) Take my yoke upon you, and learn from me, *for I am gentle and lowly in heart*, and you will find rest for your souls. (30) For my yoke is easy, and my burden is light.

We are to learn to have wisdom like the Messiah – wisdom that strives to maintain the attitude of meekness. By the way, this is not merely a suggestion, but a command. It's an imperative in the Aramaic text. We *must* follow the Messiah's example and become like Him. This is in perfect accord with Ya'akov's instructions.

---

152 TDNT, Vol. 7, "Sophos, Sophia" pg. 467

153 Mageira, "ܡܟܝܟܘܬܐ " Dict. No: 1355

> **James 3:14 MGI** But if you have bitter envy or contention in your hearts, do not elevate yourselves above the truth and lie...

Directly preceding this verse, Ya'akov gave instructions that the leader of a congregation must have a wisdom which is "*humble or lowly, meek.*" Here, he's saying that what keeps leaders from being humble is to "*become puffed up, proud, boasting or to elevate [oneself]*"[154] over the truth.

Well, the question then is this: What or Whom is ultimately the truth? However you phrase the question, the answer is the same: God! God is truth. We can observe principles in creation itself which prove that there is such a thing as "truth." There are natural laws which govern the known creation. These laws can be clarified, quantified, and verified as being "true."

There are spiritual laws as well which, through observation, can be summed up through human logic and principles. Truth can be found in creation, because creation bears the fingerprint of the Creator who is truth! Isaiah reminds us of this:

> **Isaiah 65:16 ESV** So that he who blesses himself in the land shall bless himself by *the God of truth*, and he who takes an oath in the land shall swear by *the God of truth;* because the former troubles are forgotten and are hidden from my eyes.

And being God, the Messiah says this about Himself:

> **John 14:6 ESV** Jesus said to him, "*I am* the way, and *the truth,* and the life. No one comes to the Father except through me.

Truth is that which has the characteristics of being, "*balanced, certain,*

---

154 Mageira, "ܐܝܕܝܕܝܕ" Dict. No: 0934

136

reality."[155] The word comes from the picture in the ancient world of something having been placed on a scale, and there, found to match up to its correct weight.[156] God is always correct in His character and in the way that He weighs our situations. He is truth! And the very reason that we can even discern what is true is because we were made in His image – the image of truth! Ya'akov now compares the wisdom that comes from God to the so-called human wisdom of men.

> **James 3:15 MGI**   ...because this wisdom does not come down from above, but is earthly, from the reasonings of the soul and from demons.

This should remind us of the contrast between the Jewish and the Greek view of wisdom – one from above (Jewish), one from below (Greek).

In later Judaism, the wisdom of Egypt was also considered to be *"wisdom from below."*[157] Earlier we learned that there were two key terms used for the leader of the congregation. According to verse thirteen, this person was to be wise and instructed, or, in Aramaic, "khekmat and reda." We can find another example with these two key terms for leader in the book of Acts.

> **Acts 7:22 ESV**   And Moses was *instructed* in all the *wisdom* of the Egyptians, and he was mighty in his words and deeds.

These two words now describe the great congregational leader, Moshe as one who was wise and instructed. Ya'akov is drawing a map to point us to the source of true wisdom.

At some point in ancient Judaism, the wisdom of Egypt became synonymous with wisdom that is from below. By using the same words to describe Moshe as the ultimate congregational leader, and saying that

---

155 See Strongs' H7189
156 See Benner entry: 2739
157 Zohar in Gen. fol. 119. 2.

true wisdom comes from above, Ya'akov is stating that Moshe's wisdom did not come from Egypt, but he received it from God!

Let's look at another example this time from the life of Daniel, and then we'll draw some conclusions.

> **Daniel 1:17-20 ESV** As for these four youths, God gave them learning and skill in all literature and wisdom, and Daniel had understanding in all visions and dreams. (18) At the end of the time, when the king had commanded that they should be brought in, the chief of the eunuchs brought them in before Nebuchadnezzar. (19) And the king spoke with them, and among all of them none was found like Daniel, Hananiah, Mishael, and Azariah. Therefore they stood before the king. (20) And in every matter of *wisdom* and *understanding* about which the king inquired of them, he found them ten times better than all the magicians and enchanters that were in all his kingdom.

Daniel is brought before the king of Babylon. The book of Acts describes Moshe as he stands before the Pharaoh. Although both were highly trained, Moshe found true wisdom comes only from above. Wisdom from below can come from these three sources:

- It's earthly. This means it's greatest concepts can never exceed the limits of good 'ole terra firma.
- It's from the "devices or reasonings of the soul." This means, not only is it limited to the thinking of this tiny planet, and further, to "humanity and our experiences."
- It is derived from demons.

We can now conclude that wisdom can be gleaned from several places and take several forms.

- From God (above)

- From earth (below)
- From Man (below)
- From demons (below).

There's something really interesting about this term for "demons." In Aramaic it's "shida."[158] This means: *a demon or an evil spirit.*[159] But wait, there's more! This ancient Aramaic seems to be related to an even older Hebrew word which is used to describe the demons of Babylon, the term is "shed."

The Theological Wordbook of the Old Testament gives us a bit of it's history:

> Undoubtedly Hebrew "shed" is to be connected with the Babylonian word shedu, a demon either good or evil. In pagan religions the line between gods and demons is not a constant one. There are demons who are beneficent and gods who are malicious. Generally speaking though, a demon was conceived as being less powerful than a god. In Mesopotamian thought, the shedu was a supernatural protective power for whose presence the gods were invoked. Specifically, the function of shedu may have been to represent the vitality of the individual, his sexual potency.[160]

So, the "shedu" can either be good or evil at any given time. At times the shedu are considered as fallen angels. At other times they're viewed as gods.

Another culture has also inherited this term for demons, but in their tongue it's pronounced "shiva." Pay close attention to the similar characteristics of the "shedu" of the Babylonians, and the "shiva" of the Hindus.

---

158 Magiera, "ܫܐܕܐ " Dict. No: 2469
159 Ibid.
160 Theological Wordbook of the Old Testament, "Shed" No: 2330

According to Cambridge Universities' Introduction to Hinduism, we see this:

> Shiva is a god of ambiguity and paradox, whose attributes include opposing themes.[161]

Shiva is sometimes viewed as good, and sometimes viewed as evil. The demons in the Babylonian religion were viewed as good and sometimes evil. The Greek gods were thought of as being exactly the same way.

Ya'akov is warning the Jewish believers, who are living amongst the culture of Hellenism, against becoming Hellenized. *"Just because the Greek philosophies sound reasonable, doesn't mean they are! Remember their source!"* Earthly wisdom, humanistic wisdom, and demonic wisdom – all of these are Hellenistic Greek philosophy in a nut shell.

Ya'akov is saying that a congregational leader is truly wise when he has God's wisdom. He will go into further detail as he describes the teachings and wisdom that comes from the Greeks for what it is, and will share its inevitable results.

James 3:16 MGI For where there is envy and contention, there also [is] confusion and everything that is evil.

The terms "envy and contention" are marks of the gods of the Greek pantheon, each one envious over the other, full of disputation, or better yet: *"controversy or contradiction."*

This describes perfectly that which came out of devotion to the differing gods, producing only endless discussions which never come to conclusions or, have any real practical life application. These worthless deliberations bring only "confusion" and "everything that is evil." (Sounds like much of our theological discussions today.) *They are*

---

161 Flood, Gavin (1996). An Introduction to Hinduism. Cambridge: Cambridge University Press. ISBN 0-521-43878-0, pg. 150.

"confusing" and they bring about *"everything that is evil."*

The phrase "everything that is evil" is the Aramaic term "bisha" which is also used as a synonym for hsatan (satan) because it literally means "*the evil.*"[162]

It makes sense. If our highest intellectual/spiritual wisdom consists merely of that which humans can know, or demons in their devious way, provide... we have a problem!

We can be the smartest mathematicians, brain surgeons, artists, philosophers, astronomers, or scientists in the world, yet without God's input, we'll never be truly wise. It is not possible for a person to lead a congregation toward the things of God unless that person possesses wisdom from God.

> **James 3:17 MGI**   Now the wisdom that is from above is pure and full of peace and humble and obedient and full of mercy and good fruits and is without division and does not respect persons.

Ya'akov has already told us that wisdom from below brings only "confusion." In this verse he shows us that wisdom from above brings "peace." This is precisely what Rabbi Sha'ul said to the Corinthian congregation who were surrounded by Hellenism:

> **1 Corinthians 14:33 ESV**   For God is not a God of confusion but of peace...

Roth points out the following:

> Ya'akov being fluent in the Hebrew Scriptures extends the power of this statement from a verse in the Tanakh which states: "The

---

162   See Magiera, "ܐܒܝܫ " Dict. No: 0220

mind (imagination) that is stayed on You, Thou will keep in perfect peace" (Isaiah 26:3). It is this "double shalom" that James is referencing but in a very clever and subtle way.[163]

Wisdom from above:

Is Perfect. The Aramaic term here is "deka" which means: *"to be pure, to purify, to cleanse, to purge, to be clean."*[164] It's related to the Hebrew term "zakah" meaning: *"to be innocent."*[165] A better way to translate this then might be: *the wisdom from above is "pure."*

Is Full of peace. In Hebrew, "umala shlama" or *"full of shalom."*[166] Or as Roth puts it, *"it's double shalom" (doubly peaceful, balanced and whole).*

Is Mild. Another way of translating "makika" would be: *"humble or meek."*[167]

Is Submissive. The Aramaic "meshtameana" indicates: *obedience.*

Is Full of Compassion. The Aramaic term is "rakhmey"[168] which is related to the Hebrew "rechame"[169] which means: *"mercy or tenderness"* and comes from the word "rechem"[170] for a mother's womb.

Brings Forth Good Fruits. Or this could be translated as it brings forth *"good harvests"* or *"good affects."*[171]

---

163 Roth, Aramaic English New Testament, Ya'akov 3:17, footnote 11.

164 Magiera, "ܐܕܟܐ" Dict. No: 0521

165 Strongs' "זכה" H2135

166 וּמַלְיָא שְׁלָמָא (Jam 3:17 PHA) PHA - Peshitto NT in Hebrew letters with Accents and Vowels

167 Magiera, "ܡܟܝܟܘܬܐ" Dict. No: 1355

168 Ibid., "ܪܚܡܐ" Dict. No: 2346

169 Strongs' "רחם" H7359

170 Strongs' "רחם" H7358

171 Magiera, "ܦܐܪܐ" Dict. No: 2016

Doesn't Divide or Cause Division. Nor does it respect certain individuals.

Now that we've taken a closer look at the characteristics of true wisdom, let's get back to Ya'akov's letter. Here, we find out that leaders had been dividing individuals into respective groups of rich or poor in the congregational meetings. Ya'akov is saying, a wise leader who is well-trained for the job and learns to listen to God doesn't act this way! He's knows better than that.

The Prophet Jeremiah says:

> **Jeremiah 9:23-24 ESV** Thus says the LORD: "Let not the wise man boast in his wisdom, let not the mighty man boast in his might, let not the rich man boast in his riches, (24) but let him who boasts boast in this, that he understands and knows me, that I am the LORD who practices steadfast love, justice, and righteousness in the earth. For in these things I delight, declares the LORD."

Finally, Ya'akov finishes this section with this:

> **James 3:18 MGI** And the fruit of justification is sown in quietness by those who serve peace.

When the scholars translated this passage into Greek they used just one word for peace, "eirene." However, the Aramaic uses two different words for peace here. The first indicates that stillness which is sown. The second is that which results because of it.

When we sow peace into life's circumstances, and make sure that it's sown deep within the rich soil of godliness, the outcome for us will be peace and wholeness no matter the circumstance. How much more so when peace is sown into a family, community, or across an entire planet?

Let me finish with these words from a sage long since past:

Midrash Rabbah - Deuteronomy V:12   Bar Kappara said: If the heavenly beings who are free from envy and hatred and rivalry are in need of peace, how much more are the lower beings, who are subject to hatred, rivalry, and envy, in need of peace. - Soncino

Chapter 14

In the previous chapter, Ya'akov showed that the "wisdom from above" brings about a host of positive attributes into our life experience. He wrote:

> **James 3:17-18 ESV**   But the wisdom from above is first pure, then peaceable, gentle, open to reason, full of mercy and good fruits, impartial and sincere. (18) And a harvest of righteousness is sown in peace by those who make peace.

Here, in his very next breath Ya'akov contrasts this to their actual situation. It's like he's saying, *"Given your current situation, your wisdom comes from somewhere else!"*

> **James 4:1-3 MGI**   From where are wars and arguments among you? Is it not from the desires that war in your members? (2) You desire and you do not have. And you perish and are zealous, yet it does not come into your hands. And you strive and cause wars, yet you have not, because you have not asked. (3) You ask and do not receive, because you ask wrongly, so that you may nourish your desires.

Ya'akov is saying, *"Take a look at your actions and you'll know whether the source of your wisdom comes from God or from the world!"*

We become like that which instructs us. Whether in morality, learning a trade, parenting, or any other discipline, we become like the source that trains us. Where does your source of training originate, above or below? Is your source television talk shows or God's Word? Are you being discipled by a true mentor, (one who is down the path further than you) or are you discipling yourself? If you're being discipled by someone else, you have the opportunity to grow at least as far as they've grown. If you disciple yourself, you'll get no further than what you know and where you're currently at. Your starting point has become your destination. Oh, you may learn more information, but without an external source of objective evaluation your insights will be no fresher than old water in a fish tank, merely recirculated without the benefit of fresh water being added. And like the fish tank, will become stale, stagnant, and unhealthy!

In the second verse, Ya'akov points back to an age-old problem: humans lust for and covet what they do not have.

We will better understand Ya'akov's point by looking more closely at the Aramaic text:

> **v.2** You desire and you do not have. And you perish and are zealous, yet it does not come into your hands. And you strive and cause wars, yet you have not, because you have not asked.

I would suggest that Ya'akov is, once again, pointing his audience back to the early chapters of Genesis. Ya'akov gives us some real hints here with the use of such terms as, "desire" and "perish"; and the idea of something "not coming into your hands." This, in turn, "causes wars," or better, "causes battles."

> **Genesis 3:6 ESV** So when the woman saw that the tree was good for food, and that it was a delight to the eyes, and that the tree was to be desired to make one wise, she took of its fruit and ate, and she also gave some to her husband who was with her, and he ate.

Just what was it that so captivated Eve? The forbidden fruit was a source of pleasure to the taste, pleasant to the eyes, and a source of "enlightenment." Ya'akov is equating the situation of the Jews in the diaspora with Eve, and the satanic influence of Hellenism with the forbidden fruit. He equates the first battle between brothers (Cain and Able) with the battles resulting from using wisdom from below.

Ya'akov says the reason for all of this strife is that they've gone to the wrong source to find wisdom.

> **v.2b-3** And you strive and cause wars, yet you have not, because you have not asked. (3) You ask and do not receive, because you ask wrongly, so that you may nourish your desires.

Here, Ya'akov is quoting Rabbi Yeshua, who taught that we should first ask God concerning our needs:

> **Matthew 7:6-11 ESV** Do not give dogs what is holy, and do not throw your pearls before pigs, lest they trample them underfoot and turn to attack you. (7) "Ask, and it will be given to you; seek, and you will find; knock, and it will be opened to you. (8) For everyone who asks receives, and the one who seeks finds, and to the one who knocks it will be opened. (9) Or which one of you, if his son asks him for bread, will give him a stone? (10) Or if he asks for a fish, will give him a serpent? (11) If you then, who are evil, know how to give good gifts to your children, how much more will your Father who is in heaven give good things to those who ask him!

Ya'akov goes on to teach against prioritizing the world as a source over God. He shows them how the world has won their hearts and replaced God.

> **James 4:4 MGI**   Adulterers, do you not know that the friendship of this world is in opposition to God? Therefore, he who wants to be a friend of this world becomes an opponent of God.

He is surely referring to what Yeshua said in the Sermon on the Mount:

> **Matthew 6:24 ESV**   No one can serve two masters, for either he will hate the one and love the other, or he will be devoted to the one and despise the other. You cannot serve God and money.

Ya'akov's point is that you can't mix your devotion! You can't share your soul with more than one master or embrace teachings from so many sources. The gathering of information is not a replacement for discipleship. Especially in the last few generations we have been handed the tradition which insists that maturity comes from data. Information is only part of the equation which makes a mature follower. However, just like in the garden we prefer to gather to ourself that which one should not possess.

> **James 4:5-6 MGI**   Or do you think that the scripture fruitlessly said: THE SPIRIT THAT LIVES IN US DESIRES WITH ENVY? (16) But our Lord has given abundant grace to us. Because of this, he said: GOD HUMBLES THE PROUD AND GIVES GRACE TO THE HUMBLE.

Here Ya'akov is referring to a section in the writings of Solomon that teaches how the wise man deals with his neighbor.

> **Proverbs 3:27-35 ESV**   Do not withhold good from those to whom it is due, when it is in your power to do it. (28) Do not say to your neighbor, "Go, and come again, tomorrow I will give it" – when you have it with you. (29) Do not plan evil against

your neighbor, who dwells trustingly beside you. (30) Do not contend with a man for no reason, when he has done you no harm. (31) Do not envy a man of violence and do not choose any of his ways, (32) for the devious person is an abomination to the LORD, but the upright are in his confidence. (33) The LORD's curse is on the house of the wicked, but he blesses the dwelling of the righteous. (34) Toward the scorners he is scornful, but to the humble he gives favor. (35) The wise will inherit honor, but fools get disgrace.

Ya'akov is attempting to discipline those who were behaving inappropriately, and to reinforce the principles of the Torah which they have been taught. This is how he advises them to fix the problem:

> **James 4:7 MGI** Therefore, be subject to God and stand against satan and he will flee from you.

Ya'akov says, as proven by what happened back in the garden, that looking to any source other than God, for anything, is beyond foolish and can only come to no good. The enemy is still using the same methods to lure believers today – he tempts, he entices, and he deceives in an attempt to steal that which God intends for our best.

The answer to their problems, and the answer to all problems is to subject ourselves to Elohim, and to make His will our will.

There is a saying amongst the Rabbis that goes like this:

> He used to say: do his will as [thou wouldst do] thine own will, so that he may do thy will as [He does] his [own] will. Set aside thy will in the face of his will, so that he may set aside the will of others before thy will.[172]

---

172 Mishna Avot 2.4 (Soncino Translation)

In simple English, make your will God's will that he may make his will your will.[173]

From the very beginning, the accuser wages war over us. He schemes to entice us away from our God. And as in the beginning, we can choose to listen to God, or we can choose to listen to the lies of the accuser and face the consequences.

The Aramaic text of verse seven indicates that the believer is to take a submissive posture before our Creator, but an active stance against the devil. The Aramaic text describes the believer rising up and standing his ground in direct opposition to this accuser. And it assures us that if we do stand our ground, he will flee from us. And that's the whole point.

As God's creatures, we are to submit ourselves to our Creator alone! We are not to pay attention to a messenger, who although higher than us, is still no more than an intermediary creature – and one who stands in direct opposition to the will of the One who created him! *(And looking at it in the light of this reality, why would you want to?)*

A key Aramaic term that I want to point out once again is the term for "submission." The term used for being "submitted" to Elohim is the term "evad." It is used of the servant of a king, or for one who works directly for the head of a household or tribe. Ya'akov uses this term in it's imperative verb form. In other words, it's not a suggestion or an option. Ya'akov is strongly directing (commanding) his congregational leaders to listen to and serve God rather than the culture or the devil.

> **James 4:8 MGI**   And come near to God and he will come near to you. Cleanse your hands, [you] sinners. Set apart your hearts, doubters of self.

---

173 JANT, pg. 433

Here, Ya'akov is referencing the act of ceremonial cleansing. David says of himself:

> **Psalms 26:6 ESV**   I wash my hands in innocence and go around your altar, O LORD...

In Judaism this hand-washing is called "netilat yadayim." There are many occasions for the washing of the hands before approaching God. This includes the touching of that which is unclean. This is certainly done when a person converts to Judaism. I believe Ya'akov is referencing both scenarios.

- He is showing that in separating the rich from the poor of the assembly, the congregational leader has become unclean by the unjust treatment of his neighbor.

- He recognizes the need for this leader to approach God as if for the first time, in repentance, humility, setting himself apart for God alone, like a conversion that is made by a proselyte.

Here are a couple examples of the priority of purity:

> **Psalms 24:4 ESV**   He who has clean hands and a pure heart, who does not lift up his soul to what is false and does not swear deceitfully.

> **Matthew 5:8 ESV**   Blessed are the pure in heart, for they shall see God.

In Judaism, the washing of the hands or feet is much more than a need for physical cleansing but is rather a symbolic act to remind a man of his need for cleansing of the inside.

When the Zohar, the mystical Jewish commentary on Leviticus was penned, the author had this to say about the words *"be holy, for I the*

Lord am holy":

> A man sanctifies himself on the earth, and then he is sanctified from heaven. As a man is a sinner, he must have his hands cleansed from wicked works; as he is double-minded, he must have his heart sanctified. Sanctification belongs to the heart, because of pollution of mind; cleansing belongs to the hands, because of sinful acts.[174]

Ya'akov seems to have had this in mind here as he speaks of this "double-mindedness" or as is sometimes translated as being "double-souled," where a person's heart is in two places at once. And because of this divided devotion, a person's morality and ethical behavior will be divided as well. We act upon what we believe. Or at least, we should act upon what we believe.

> **Isaiah 1:15-19 ESV**   When you spread out your hands, I will hide my eyes from you; even though you make many prayers, I will not listen; your hands are full of blood. (16) Wash yourselves; make yourselves clean; remove the evil of your deeds from before my eyes; cease to do evil, (17) learn to do good; seek justice, correct oppression; bring justice to the fatherless, plead the widow's cause. (18) "Come now, let us reason together, says the LORD: though your sins are like scarlet, they shall be as white as snow; though they are red like crimson, they shall become like wool. (19) If you are willing and obedient, you shall eat the good of the land...

And as a person turns back to God, there should be an intense realization that, just as our first parents fell through pride, we should reject our pride and come humbly before our Creator.

---

174 Zohar, Lev. vol. 33, col. 132

> **James 4:9 MGI**   Humble yourselves and mourn. And your laughter will be changed to mourning and your joy to sorrow.

We can see this same principle in Master Yeshua's words:

> **Matthew 5:4 ESV**   Blessed are those who mourn, for they shall be comforted.

Ya'akov now shows the benefit of becoming low before God:

> **James 4:10 MGI**   Humble yourselves before the LORD and he will elevate you.

Amazingly, when we recognize our proper position as the creation before the Creator, God takes us from our properly low position and lifts us up so that we might have fellowship with Him who is above all others!

These words were written in the second century BCE:

> If you live in accord with the Lord's commands, God will exalt you with good things forever.[175]

---

175 Testament of the Twelve Patriarchs, Joseph 18.1 Charlesworth, Old Testament Pseudepigrapha vol II, pg 823

Chapter 15

Our last chapter showed that the person who truly seeks wisdom is the one who puts his relationship with God above all else. This man recognizes his need to approach God in humility with a pure heart, and therefore, mourns over his sin.

Ya'akov has been discussing how the very source of quarrels and fights come from pride and covetousness. Rebellion stems from nothing less than vain pride! He has referred us back to the decision in the garden: either follow God's will and live, or, like the accuser, follow your own will in outright rebellion against your Creator. Serve God and be free or you'll end up serving the accuser as a slave to sin.

Ya'akov now shows some of the obvious problems caused by pride:

> **James 4:11 MGI** Do not speak against one another, my brothers, for he who speaks against his brother or judges his brother, speaks against the law and judges the law. And if you judge the law, you are not a doer of the law, but its judge.

Is this not the exact chain of events which took place in the garden with the evil one? Didn't he speak against God's character by questioning His motives and words?

By this, Ya'akov says of their current situation that they are speaking against each other which in turn is ultimately speaking against God's Torah.

Back in the garden, God's instructions were spoken against by the accuser. Here, Ya'akov tells the assembly that they are doing the very same thing. By judging one other, they are speaking against God's instructions. It's quite obvious from which source this worldly wisdom derived. Ya'akov wants his fellow Jews to understand where this originates and where it will lead. satan, hasatan – the adversary and accuser – has continued to keep humanity at a distance from its Creator through promoting the sin of pride and self-centeredness.

Once again, Ya'akov refers to Yeshua's teaching:

> **Matthew 7:1-5** Judge not, that you be not judged. (2) For with the judgment you pronounce you will be judged, and with the measure you use it will be measured to you. (3) Why do you see the speck that is in your brother's eye, but do not notice the log that is in your own eye? (4) Or how can you say to your brother, 'Let me take the speck out of your eye,' when there is the log in your own eye? (5) You hypocrite, first take the log out of your own eye, and then you will see clearly to take the speck out of your brother's eye.

I think His words are very clear: *Get rid of the weeds from your own backyard before attempting to inspect the weeds in your brothers' yard.*

> **James 4:12 MGI** There is one lawgiver and judge, who is able to give life and to destroy. But who are you that you are judging your neighbor?

Translation: *When you judge others you attempt to take on the role that belongs solely to God!* Yeshua often reminds us concerning the respect one should have for God. Look at what he said here in Matthew's gospel:

> **Matthew 10:28** And do not fear those who kill the body but cannot kill the soul. Rather fear him who can destroy both soul and body in hell.

Rabbi Sha'ul would write:

> **Hebrews 12:28-29 ESV**   Therefore let us be grateful for receiving a kingdom that cannot be shaken, and thus let us offer to God acceptable worship, with reverence and awe, (29) for our God is a consuming fire.

Sh'lomo said:

> **Ecclesiastes 5:7 ESV**   For when dreams increase and words grow many, there is vanity; but God is the one you must fear.

Ya'akov reminds us that we have a reason to remain humble, because there will be a coming One who will bring judgment.

I can't help but mention that which is most obvious to me. The Torah is the standard by which man is judged. And Ya'akov's point is that it's utterly ridiculous to place ourselves as judge over He who is the ultimate judge over us. Whenever we take it upon ourselves to judge others, we do just that.

It is written in the Mishnah:

> Judah b. Tabbai and Simeon b. Shetah received [the oral tradition] from them [i.e. the foregoing]. Judah b. Tabbai said: do thou not [as-a judge] play the part of an advocate; whilst they [i.e. the parties in a lawsuit] are standing before thee, let them be regarded by thee as if they were [both of them] guilty, and when they leave thy presence, [after] having submitted to the judgment let them be regarded by thee as if they were [both of them] guiltless.[176]

We must judge each person by the same scale, and give the benefit of the doubt to every person. In the Talmud under the section concerning

---

176 Mas. Avot 1.8

Shabbat we read a similar bit of advice:

> Our Rabbis taught: He who judges his neighbor in the scale of merit is himself judged favorably.[177]

In other words, judge favorably and you'll be favorably judged. Ya'akov continues regarding the pride of humanity:

> **James 4:13-14 MGI** Now what will we also say about those who say, "Today or tomorrow we will go to a certain city and we will work there [for] one year and we will do business and increase?" (14) And they do not know what will happen tomorrow. For what is our life, except a vapor that is seen a little while and [then] vanishes and is gone?

Here Ya'akov is addressing the sin of presumption. First, he says we're presumptuous in our judgment over each other. Now, he says we're even being presumptuous in our judgment over our own lives, for we even presume to know what our future will hold. The bottom-line is we just think too highly of ourselves. We have the tendency toward leaving God the Creator out of the equation. For only God knows how to perfectly judge, and only God knows what will happen to us tomorrow!

The origin of this scriptural principle seems to come from the writer of Proverbs who said:

> **Proverbs 27:1 ESV** Do not boast about tomorrow, for you do not know what a day may bring.

Compare this with what Yeshua said in His Sermon on the Mount. He is discussing the impossibility of serving two masters, similar to Ya'akov discussing the incompatibility of the two types of wisdom.

---

177 Talmud, Shabbat 127b

Matthew 6:24-34 ESV No one can serve two masters, for either he will hate the one and love the other, or he will be devoted to the one and despise the other. You cannot serve God and money. (25) Therefore I tell you, do not be anxious about your life, what you will eat or what you will drink, nor about your body, what you will put on. Is not life more than food, and the body more than clothing? (26) Look at the birds of the air: they neither sow nor reap nor gather into barns, and yet your heavenly Father feeds them. Are you not of more value than they? (27) And which of you by being anxious can add a single hour to his span of life? (28) And why are you anxious about clothing? Consider the lilies of the field, how they grow: they neither toil nor spin, (29) yet I tell you, even Solomon in all his glory was not arrayed like one of these. (30) But if God so clothes the grass of the field, which today is alive and tomorrow is thrown into the oven, will he not much more clothe you, O you of little faith? (31) Therefore do not be anxious, saying, 'What shall we eat?' or 'What shall we drink?' or 'What shall we wear?' (32) For the Gentiles seek after all these things, and your heavenly Father knows that you need them all. (33) But seek first the kingdom of God and his righteousness, and all these things will be added to you. (34) Therefore do not be anxious about tomorrow, for tomorrow will be anxious for itself. Sufficient for the day is its own trouble.

Further, The practice of presuming to know what the days ahead would hold was strongly criticized by the Rabbis of the day. They taught that tomorrow's prospects may never come, for one never knows what tomorrow will bring! Here is one illustration from the Talmud:

> [They were] like a man who was kept in prison and people told him: Tomorrow, they will release you from the prison and give you plenty of money. And he answered them: I pray of you, let me go free today and I shall ask nothing more!

Similarly, Rabbi Yosef taught:

Fret not over tomorrow's trouble, for thou knowest not what a day may bring forth, and peradventure tomorrow he is no more: thus he shall be found grieving over a world that is not his.[178]

There's a great story contained in the Midrash Rabbah on Deuteronomy (Ya'akov may have had this very story in mind). This story speaks for itself:

Our Rabbis said: Once R. Simeon b. Halafta went to a circumcision ceremony. The father of the child made a feast and gave those present wine seven years old to drink, he also said: 'Of this wine, I will store away a portion for my son's wedding feast.' The feast continued until midnight. R. Simeon b. Halafta, who trusted in his own [moral] strength, left at midnight to return to his city. On the road, the Angel of Death met him and R. Simeon noticed he was looking strange. He asked him: 'Who are you?' And the latter answered: 'I am God's messenger.' He asked him: ' Why are you looking strange?' He replied: 'On account of the talk of human beings who say: "This and that we will do," and yet not one of them knows when he will be summoned to die. The man in whose feast you have shared, and who said to you: "Of this wine I will store away a portion for my son's wedding feast," lo, his [child's] time has come, he is to be snatched away after thirty days.'[179]

This phrase used by Ya'akov in verse thirteen, *"Today or tomorrow we will go to a certain city and we will work there [for] one year and we will do business and increase"* seems to be referring to a custom of the day. Adam Clarke notes the following:

The custom of those ancient times; they traded from city to city, carrying their goods on the backs of camels. The Jews traded thus to Tyre, Sidon, Caesarea, Crete, Ephesus, Philippi, Thessalonica, Corinth, Rome, etc. And it is to this kind of

178 Ibid., Babylonian Talmud, Sanhedrin 100b
179 Midrash Rabbah - Deuteronomy IX:1 (Soncino Edition)

itinerant mercantile life that St. James alludes.[180]

This was a common form of speech being used by his Jewish brothers whereby they would forecast their commerce a year in advance. Ya'akov says this is a foolish way for us to view our lives. We are to focus instead on serving God today and trust Him for our tomorrow.

> **Matthew 6:31-32 ESV** Therefore do not be anxious, saying, 'What shall we eat?' or 'What shall we drink?' or 'What shall we wear?' (32) For the Gentiles seek after all these things...

Were these Jews who were living among the Gentiles being influenced by the Gentiles? Absolutely!

> **v.14b** ...for what is our life but a vapor that is seen a little while and then vanishes and is gone?

This is a common Hebrew phrase which was used by Job and the prophets of old, and to which Ya'akov alluded in chapter 1:11.

> **Job 7:6-7 ESV** My days are swifter than a weaver's shuttle and come to their end without hope. (7) Remember that my life is a breath; my eye will never again see good.

And David writes:

> **Psalms 39:5 ESV** Behold, you have made my days a few handbreadths, and my lifetime is as nothing before you. Surely all mankind stands as a mere breath! Selah.

Many of the prophets used a similar form of this phrase. The thought that our lives are as short as a breath has been inspirational within Judaism. And it's a familiar Jewish term that Ya'akov uses when he

---

180 Adam Clarke, commentary on James 4:13

writes, *"what is our life?"*

In the Talmud, in section Yoma 87b, we read the lengthy discussion on how the phrase *"what is our life?"* was added to the end of prayers to signify that only God knows what the future holds for us! This is still a relevant question for each of us today. What is our life?

Ya'akov then offers the correct way we should view our existence:

> **James 4:15 MGI**   Instead, they should say, "If the LORD wills and we live, we will do this or that."

Once again, tradition would have made this a common remark among first-century Jews. Rabbi Sha'ul uses the same phraseology in his letters:

> **Acts 18:21 ESV**   But on taking leave of them he said, "I will return to you *if God wills,*" and he set sail from Ephesus.

> **1 Corinthians 4:19 ESV**   But I will come to you soon, *if the Lord wills,* and I will find out not the talk of these arrogant people but their power.

This is exactly what the Messiah taught by the way that He lived His life.

> **Matthew 26:39 ESV**   And going a little farther he fell on his face and prayed, saying, "My Father, if it be possible, let this cup pass from me; nevertheless, *not as I will, but as you will.*"

This same sentiment is echoed throughout the Talmud:

> R. Alexandri on concluding his prayer added the following: *May it be Thy will,* O Lord our God, to station us in an illumined corner and do not station us in a darkened corner, and let not our heart be sick nor our eyes darkened! According to some this

161

was the prayer of R. Hamnuna, and R. Alexandri on concluding his prayer used to add the following: Sovereign of the Universe, it is known full well to Thee that our will is to perform Thy will, and what prevents us? The yeast in the dough and the subjection to the foreign Powers. *May it be Thy will* to deliver us from their hand, so that we may return to perform the statutes of Thy will with a perfect heart![181]

> **James 4:16 MGI** They boast in their pride. All boasting like this is evil.

The Aramaic word used here translated as "boast" or in some translations as "glory" is the word "beher" which literally means: "*to shine, be bright*."[182] The idea here is that the person who focuses on himself attempts to make himself the most observable to those around him. (*Hey! Look at me!*) Ya'akov says that the person who is self-important is merely pointing out his own arrogance. (*Hey! See how prideful I am!*)

Ya'akov says that this type of self-importance comes from "evil," which is "be-ish" in Aramaic and comes from the Hebrew term which means "*to smell bad*." Evil is a stench in the nostrils of the righteous!

We've been instructed as to what is to be our position before God, and we are held responsible to do what we know.

> **James 4:17 MGI** And he who knows good and does not do it, to him it is sin.

In the parable of the unfaithful servant, Yeshua concludes:

Luke 12:47 ESV And that servant who knew his master's will

---

181   Babylonian Talmud, Berachot 17a

182   Magiera, "ܒܗܪ" Dict No: 0231 Also compare Jennings, p. 214

but did not get ready or act according to his will, will receive a severe beating.

The same conclusion can be found in the Parable of the Sheep and the Goats, where the goats on the left are told:

> **Matthew 25:41-46 ESV** Then he will say to those on his left, 'Depart from me, you cursed, into the eternal fire prepared for the devil and his angels. (42) For I was hungry and you gave me no food, I was thirsty and you gave me no drink, (43) I was a stranger and you did not welcome me, naked and you did not clothe me, sick and in prison and you did not visit me.' (44) Then they also will answer, saying, 'Lord, when did we see you hungry or thirsty or a stranger or naked or sick or in prison, and did not minister to you?' (45) Then he will answer them, saying, 'Truly, I say to you, as you did not do it to one of the least of these, you did not do it to me.' (46) And these will go away into eternal punishment, but the righteous into eternal life.

All these knew what was right to do, yet didn't do it and were punished. The Rabbis of the day taught the same:

> Whoever can forbid his household [to commit a sin] but does not, is seized for [the sins of] his household; [if he can forbid] his fellow citizens, he is seized for [the sins of] his fellow citizens; if the whole world, he is seized for [the sins of] the whole world.[183]

Although God forbid mankind to sin, from the very beginning until now, He allowed *Himself* to be seized for the sins of the whole world.

> **John 3:16 ESV** For God so loved the world, that he gave his only Son, that whoever believes in him should not perish but have eternal life.

---

183   Babylonian Talmud, Shabbat 15b (Soncino Edition)

Chapter 16

Chapter fifteen brought us the clear message the we are held responsible to enact the things we know. What then do we know?

We know that it's imperative that we look to God only as the source of everything – for his wisdom, for our provisions for the day, and for our tomorrow. We know better than to speak ill of or to judge another person. We know that we are to be quick to listen, slow to speak, and that our speech, when we do speak, should be sweet (edifying). We know that we mustn't show favoritism. We know that the worldly ways of thinking only lead us down the wrong road and away from God. We know that faith separated from action is no faith at all. We know that true faith lives out what it inwardly believes. And finally, we know that in all these things we will be held accountable before God.

As Ya'akov puts the finishing lines on the final page of this letter, we find him drawing conclusions.

> **James 5:1 MGI**   Oh rich [men], wail and weep for the miseries that will come on you...

Ya'akov is clearly connecting the dots and taking us back to where he began the letter, with distinctions being made between the rich and the poor believers. This would be most important, given the extreme poverty much of the believing community was experiencing at that time.

To the rich believers he gives two commands: *"to wail"* and *"to weep."*[184] Both are imperatives in the Aramaic text. "To wail" is "yilel" which is: *a picture of someone who in extreme grief is seen "howling."* It's the Aramaic term used for a wolf howling during the dark night.[185] This term for howling is related to the night or darkness, and is on the hunt, in search of prey. What a vivid picture Ya'akov paints for us of the rich person who sees his impoverished brother merely as a way to meet his own needs! He sees these ones who have heaped up wealth to themselves and have not helped their poor brothers as being in the dark, howling. Experts on wolf behavior tell us that wolves howl in order to gather, strengthen, or reestablish their pack. And this would be exactly what was needed for a group divided by financial standing. These believers had allowed their "pack" to become weakened through divisions and favoritism of the rich.

This message has a double meaning. The first: *"Yes, howl to call your pack back together and reestablish your congregation."*

The picture is further amplified through his next choice of words: *"to weep."* This Aramaic word "beka" has the following meanings: *weep, cry, lament, bewail.*[186] Beka comes from the Hebrew root "bakah" which indicates the weeping and tears which come from *"remorse or repentance."*[187]

The Theological Wordbook of the Old Testament explains:

> "whereas tears are associated with the eyes, weeping (*bakah*) is associated with the voice; Semites do not weep quietly, but aloud."[188]

---

184 For the Aramaic see Magiera, "ᴸᴸ" #1052. For it's Hebrew equivalent see Strong's # H3213
185 See AHLB #1265
186 For the Aramaic see Magiera "ᴷᴬᴬ" #0267. For it's Hebrew equivalent see Strong's # H1058
187 TWOT "" #0243
188 Ibid.

Therefore, accompanying this need to restore the breach in the pack, is also the necessity to recognize one's personal responsibility for its division. Ya'akov says, in effect, *"You're personally responsible for this. You have caused this to happen. Now fix it! Repent over it! Let others hear your deep pain over the pain you've caused others!"*

He says that they should do this:

> **v.1** for the miseries that will come on you...

Then, like we saw in chapter one, Ya'akov returns to the topic of the divisions caused by wealth.

> **James 5:2 MGI** ...for your wealth is corrupted and is rotten and your garments have been eaten by a moth.

There's a lot going on in this verse, so it's important to get the overall picture. Ya'akov equates accumulated wealth that is not being used to help the poor with clothing that is stored away and eaten by moths. It benefits no one.

This theme is also found in other books of the Bible. Here are a couple examples:

> **Matthew 6:19-21 ESV** Do not lay up for yourselves treasures on earth, where moth and rust destroy and where thieves break in and steal, (20) but lay up for yourselves treasures in heaven, where neither moth nor rust destroys and where thieves do not break in and steal. (21) For where your treasure is, there your heart will be also.

> **Job 13:28 ESV** Man wastes away like a rotten thing, like a garment that is moth-eaten.

166

The word Ya'akov uses for "rotten" is "kheval" which has the meaning of that which: "*causes hurt, or destruction.*"[189] Wealth is being viewed here like a piece of fruit that has gone bad. When the need was there, had it been given, it could have perfectly met the need. But since it was withheld, it became rotten and was no longer of value to nourish anyone. It should have been used to feed the "pack," yet they starved and were forced to look elsewhere. Ya'akov is saying that it is this worldly and selfish mindset that is destroying the congregation.

By the way, "kheval" is also used to describe the intense kind of pain a woman feels during childbirth.[190]

Can you fathom the pain of a parent unable to feed their child, when there was a fellow believer in their own assembly who could have helped, but looked the other way? And the resources of the wealthy to which Ya'akov is referring is not limited to "garments," but is the Aramaic word "mana" which is used to denote possessions of any kind.[191]

Ya'akov is directing the leaders to instruct the wealthy of the congregation to use their means to help those without. Clearly, he says that when used for any other purpose, wealth is of no value at all. This is by no means a slam to those who were wealthy, but a condemnation of the selfish hoarding of that which could help others.

> **James 5:3 MGI**   And your gold and your silver have tarnished and their tarnish will be a witness against you and it is going to eat your flesh. You have gathered a fire for you for the last days.

Maybe Ya'akov had this verse in mind when penning his words:

---

189   See BDB "חבל" #H2255
190   See Magiera "ܚܒܠ" #0702
191   Ibid., "ܡܐܢܐ" #1320

Proverbs 1:18-19 ESV   ...but these men lie in wait for their own blood; they set an ambush for their own lives. (19) Such are the ways of everyone who is greedy for unjust gain; it takes away the life of its possessors.

In God's opinion, holding onto wealth rather than using it to help a brother is extremely offensive. Righteousness (tzedekah) is the motivation or means by which we attempt to level the playing field for all people. What Ya'akov is describing here is just the opposite. This common behavior produces three shocking things:

- It is a witness (gives testimony) against you.
- It will eat (devour) your flesh.
- You have gathered (stacked, heaped up) fire for you for the last days.

Rabbi Sha'ul spoke about this attitude and the results it will produce when he wrote to the Romans:

Romans 2:5 ESV   But because of your hard and impenitent heart you are storing up wrath for yourself on the day of wrath when God's righteous judgment will be revealed.

We're judged upon the merit of what is and isn't righteous. Ya'akov says that the unrighteous acts that we do will testify against us, and will become firewood for the coming fiery judgment against us.

Compare Paul's wordss to the Corinthians:

1 Corinthians 3:12-15 ESV   Now if anyone builds on the foundation with gold, silver, precious stones, wood, hay, straw – (13) each one's work will become manifest, for the Day will disclose it, because it will be revealed by fire, and the fire will test what sort of work each one has done. (14) If the work that anyone has built on the foundation survives, he will receive a reward. (15) If anyone's work is burned up, he will suffer loss, though he himself will be saved, but only as through fire.

> **James 5:4 MGI** Behold, the wage of the laborers who have reaped your lands, which you have withheld, cries out. And the crying of the reapers has entered the ears of the LORD of Hosts.

Here, Ya'akov is pointing his Jewish brothers back to the Torah, the instruction manual, saying: *"You know better than this. Look! It has been written down for you that you might study and know it, and you still don't do it!"*

This is in reference to Deuteronomy:

> **Deuteronomy 24:14-15 ESV** You shall not oppress a hired worker who is poor and needy, whether he is one of your brothers or one of the sojourners who are in your land within your towns. (15) You shall give him his wages on the same day, before the sun sets (for he is poor and counts on it), lest he cry against you to the LORD, and you be guilty of sin.

Ya'akov is pointing to the fact that day-laborers were laboring but their pay was being withheld for whatever reason.[192] God had already given instructions warning against this unfair practice.

The Prophet Jeremiah spoke out against this practice as well.

> **Jeremiah 22:13 ESV** Woe to him who builds his house by unrighteousness, and his upper rooms by injustice, who makes his neighbor serve him for nothing and does not give him his wages...

---

192 For further explanation see frucktenbaum's commentary, pg. 299

So did Malachi:

> **Malachi 3:5 ESV**   Then I will draw near to you for judgment. I will be a swift witness against the sorcerers, against the adulterers, against those who swear falsely, against those who oppress the hired worker in his wages, the widow and the fatherless, against those who thrust aside the sojourner, and do not fear me, says the LORD of hosts.

> Ya'akov's example was intended to hit hard. These believers were going directly against God's Word! They were living unrighteous lives like the pagans. They had become like the unbelieving, self-absorbed world of the diaspora who were drenched in ego-centric Hellenism. And while living in a foreign land, they had forsaken the lifestyle that is expected from subjects of the King of the Universe!

By the way, this verse marks the only time a New Testament writer incorporates the term "Lord of Hosts" (literally, "Lord of Sabbaths") in his writing. Rabbi Sha'ul uses it once, but only in that he's quoting from Isaiah 1:9.

> **Romans 9:29 ESV**   And as Isaiah predicted, "If the *Lord of hosts* had not left us offspring, we would have been like Sodom and become like Gomorrah."

What does that mean? Simply put, "MarYah Tsevauth," which means: *Almighty God (YHVH) of Armies (hosts)*! MarYah is the One who commands the heavenly armies. In as much as the cries of the enslaved Hebrews entered into the ears of the Lord, the cries of his people who are being financially oppressed enters into His ears as well.

In effect, Ya'akov is saying: *"God can call down armies to straighten this out. So, think about changing how you're living and stop treating each another so shamefully!"*

Chapter 17

In the last chapter, Ya'akov was teaching specifically in regard to the problems plaguing these believing Jews while living in the diaspora. They had become like the world in which they lived – taking advantage of the poor in their congregations. The older brother of the Lord was rebuking them and reminding them to return to the teaching of the Torah. This is where we pick up the text:

> **James 5:5 MGI** For you have lived in pleasure on the earth and have been greedy and have nourished your bodies as in the day of slaughter.

Here, Ya'akov explains that by their self-serving behavior they have "*reveled*" and "*feasted*," growing spiritually fat, like a Thanksgiving turkey.

Here's a few of the Aramaic words in Ya'akov's description: "you have lived in pleasure" is "besem" which means: "*to be merry, to be sweet, to have delight.*" It's even a word used for the perfume of the day.[193] So, Ya'akov is saying that these wealthy believers are enjoying the sweet life. Even though their brothers are living a tortured existence before their very eyes, they do nothing to stop it. It doesn't even affect them because they are insulated by their wealth.

The Aramaic term for "lived" or "reveled" is "leab" which means: "*to be greedy; to indulge the appetite.*"[194] The next term "nourished" or "to feast" is the Aramaic word "tarsi." This word means: to "*support, feed, nourish,*

---

193 Magiera, "ܒܣܡ" #0286

194 Ibid., "ܠܥܒ" #1307

171

sustain, provide."[195] This term is related to the practice of "*the fattening of an ox,*" or "*the feeding of cattle.*"[196] Ya'akov says the wealthy by their self-serving behavior, are preparing themselves as if for their own slaughter. Whenever a person is fattened, in the Hebrew perspective, they become numb to poverty and callused to the welfare of the people around them.

Here's an example of this usage from the Psalms:

> **Psalms 119:69-70 ESV** The insolent smear me with lies, but with my whole heart I keep your precepts; (70) their heart is unfeeling like fat, but I delight in your law (*Torah*).

Their feasting and self-indulgence is seen as fat which insulates them from the poverty around them. And this is the key division which had crept into the congregations in the diaspora. How could this happen? They had become just like the world around them! They had taken on the characteristics and behaviors of the Gentile world. They had forsaken the ethical standards for living they had learned from God's instructions. These were Jews, so we know that they had been taught how to love God and to love others. However, the influences of Hellenism had crept in and clouded their spiritual standards. They had become like the gentiles they were called to reach!

By using the phrase "*as in a day of slaughter,*" Ya'akov reveals that he probably had in mind the words of Jeremiah, who was like Ya'akov, in that he was revered in his day:

> **Jeremiah 25:34 ESV** Wail, you shepherds, and cry out, and roll in ashes, you lords of the flock, *for the days of your slaughter* and dispersion have come, and you shall fall like a choice vessel.

Here, Jeremiah is using the same tone – condemning those in positions of influence for their behavior.

---

195 Ibid., "ܠܒܘܣ" #2715
196 Payne Smith's Syriac Dictionary, pg. 621

Here is a similar expression of *"to wail"* and *"to cry out,"* which Ya'akov used in verse one:

James 5:1 Murdock O ye rich ones, wail and weep, on account of the miseries that are coming upon you.

> **James 5:6 MGI** You have condemned and killed the Just [one] and he did not stand against you.

The "you" here is plural. Ya'akov is addressing the congregations as a whole. But, who is "the Just one?" Well, "the Just one" here is singular. As Ariel Fruchtenbaum points out:

If the word righteous *(or just)* is used of a singular person, then it refers to the Messiah, Who is the Righteous One.[197]

Interestingly, this is the exact title that would be used for Ya'akov after his death. He would become known as Ya'akov HaTsaddik (James the Righteous).

Tsaddik is used of the Messiah in many places in scripture. Here are but a few examples:

Acts 3:14 ESV But you denied the *Holy and Righteous One,* and asked for a murderer to be granted to you,

Acts 7:52 ESV Which of the prophets did your fathers not persecute? And they killed those who announced beforehand the coming of *the Righteous One,* whom you have now betrayed and murdered,

1 John 2:1 ESV My little children, I am writing these things to you so that you may not sin. But if anyone does sin, we have an

---

197 Fruchtenbaum, pg. 301

advocate with the Father, *Jesus Christ the righteous.*

It is also possible that Ya'akov is grouping all of the righteous together as though they were just one. If so, then his point is that the wealthy are suppressing their kinsmen, just as the Messiah was oppressed by his kinsmen. And in the same way that He did not resist, neither do they. The tsaddikim are allowing themselves to be suppressed in order to practice the righteousness of The Righteous One. However, I tend to agree with Fruchtenbaum's conclusion that Ya'akov is speaking of the Messiah in this verse.

Ya'akov says, in affect, *"You people of influence are doing the same thing to your brothers as the people of influence did to our Lord!" You're condemning and murdering them just as He was condemned and murdered!"*

Ya'akov continues:

> **James 5:7 MGI**   But you, my brothers, be long-suffering until the coming of the LORD, as the farmer who waits for the precious fruit of his ground and is long-suffering about it, until he receives the early and latter rain.

The term *my brothers* tells us that Ya'akov is now directing these words not to the wealthy, but to the righteous who are being oppressed. It is the righteous ones with whom Ya'akov sympathizes. He advises them to have patience. The Aramaic phrase used here for "Long-suffering" is: "negar rhukha" or *"long spirited."* It means: *"to possess an enduring spirit."* In physical terms, it would mean to *"to take in or hold a deep breath."*

Here are a few questions for you. Spiritually, how long can you hold your breath? Are you taking in full lungs of oxygen each time that you pray, every time that you study scripture? Are you taking in deep breaths of the Spirit of God so that you able to wait on the bottom at the deep end of circumstances until the Messiah returns and you can come up for air?

Ya'akov uses the same imagery as before of the land that is worked. When he used this example previously, it was to condemn the wealthy for not paying the workers. Now, Ya'akov turns this example around and puts the oppressed in the position of the farmer. He's saying, in effect,

"Just like the farmer is waiting for his crops to produce and be harvested, so in the same way should you wait for your righteousness to produce a harvest."

The rich literally own the land that the oppressed are working, yet Ya'akov sees the oppressed believers as being the landowners who, themselves, will bear the fruit. He assures that they will be compensated for their labors. They will eventually be paid for all their work.

When will this happen? How long will they have to wait?

> **v.7b** ...until he receives the early and latter rain.

The phrase "the early and latter rain" was a well-known reference by the rabbis to the coming of the Messiah.

So, the humble and oppressed believers are to be patient for the coming of the Messiah, just as the farmer is patient for the coming rain. In Israel, the early rain comes sometime during the months of October and November, and the latter rain usually comes in the months of March and April. This natural occurrence is mentioned several times in scripture:

Deuteronomy 11:13-14 ESV And if you will indeed obey my commandments that I command you today, to love the LORD your God, and to serve him with all your heart and with all your soul, (14) he will give the rain for your land in its season, the early rain and the later rain, that you may gather in your grain and your wine and your oil.

175

Jeremiah 5:24 ESV They do not say in their hearts, 'Let us fear the LORD our God, who gives the rain in its season, the autumn rain and the spring rain, and keeps for us the weeks appointed for the harvest.'

Joel 2:23 ESV Be glad, O children of Zion, and rejoice in the LORD your God, for he has given the early rain for your vindication; he has poured down for you abundant rain, the early and the latter rain, as before.

Hosea links the "former and latter rains" to the coming of Messiah:

Hosea 6:1-3 ESV Come, let us return to the LORD; for he has torn us, that he may heal us; he has struck us down, and he will bind us up. (2) After two days he will revive us; on the third day he will raise us up, that we may live before him. (3) Let us know; let us press on to know the LORD; his going out is sure as the dawn; he will come to us as the showers, as the spring rains that water the earth.

Both the early and the latter rain occur during the two main periods of the Jewish feasts. The key events in the first advent, the salvific work of the Messiah, have taken place on the exact days of the feasts. This is the "early rain" of which Ya'akov is speaking. When the Messiah returns, we can fully expect that this "latter rain" will fall on the precise days of the feasts as well.

Ya'akov is saying, "The rains are coming again. Make sure your fields are ready!" This leads us to his next instruction:

> **James 5:9 MGI** Do not murmur against one another, my brothers, so that you should not be judged, for behold, judgment stands before the door.

While being patient and waiting for the Lord, Ya'akov wants those under his leadership to follow through with all of his instructions from the earlier parts of the letter. This is a warning to avoid all the consequences addressed in each of the previous chapters. In this verse, the word translated as "murmur" means: to "*groan, sigh deeply or murmur.*"[198] This word is used for the sound that cattle make.[199] And seeing that Ya'akov just used the same imagery when he spoke of them fattening themselves up like cattle, it makes total sense. In effect, Ya'akov is saying *"You're not only acting like cows (getting ready for the slaughter), but you sound like them too! You're mooing against one another!"*

By the way, cows moo when they're unhappy. A happy cow is a silent cow. Therefore, when they're distressed, in fear of danger, hungry, or in pain... they moo!

Riches do not make a person happy! An obedient relationship with God does!

Wise King Solomon said:

> **Proverbs 1:19 ESV**   Such are the ways of everyone who is greedy for unjust gain; it takes away the life of its possessors.

Regarding judging one another, the Torah describes very specifically who it is that is the final judge.

> **Genesis 18:25 ESV**   Far be it from you to do such a thing, to put the righteous to death with the wicked, so that the righteous fare as the wicked! Far be that from you! Shall not the Judge of all the earth do what is just?

Ya'akov is repeating almost exactly what Rabbi Yeshua had preached:

---

198 Magiera, " ܐܢܩ " #0125
199 Brown, Driver, Brigg's #584 אָנַח

Matthew 7:1-2 ESV   Judge not, that you be not judged.(2) For with the judgment you pronounce you will be judged, and with the measure you use it will be measured to you.

We find this same teaching in the Babylonian Talmud:

> In the measure with which a man measures it is meted out to him. She adorned herself for a transgression; the Holy One, blessed be He, made her repulsive. She exposed herself for a transgression; the Holy One, blessed be He, held her up for exposure. She began the transgression with the thigh and afterwards with the womb; therefore she is punished first in the thigh and afterwards in the womb, nor does all the body escape.[200]

Now, let's examine Ya'akov's final comment in verse nine:

---

v.9b   behold, judgment stands before the door.

Once again, this is a reiteration of the warning Ya'akov gave back in chapter four. It's this ongoing repetition of specific directions that was the method by which Jewish children learned to keep the Torah. This continues throughout a Jew's lifetime, as adults hear the Torah each week in synagogue.

But what does this statement about *"judgment standing before the door"* mean? This is another Hebraic phrase which takes the reader all the way back to the early pages of Genesis, where this type of phrase first appears. The story is the follow-up on Cain's sin against his brother Abel. After God reproves Cain for the murder of his brother we read these words:

Genesis 4:6-7 ESV   The LORD said to Cain, "Why are you

---

200 Babylonian Talmud, m. Sotah 1.7

angry, and why has your face fallen? (7) If you do well, will you not be accepted? And if you do not do well, sin is crouching at the door. Its desire is for you, but you must rule over it."

Very similar words are used in both the Genesis text and Ya'akov's letter. Both sections contain the language and imagery of the offering of "fat."[201] Both sections have to do with being reproved for the wrongs done to a brother. And both sections contain the imagery of a door.

In the Genesis story, the fat portion was offered up to God. Leviticus reveals that the fat portions were always to be offered up to God. They were His alone.

In Ya'akov's letter, he openly criticizes the wealthy for "feasting" (fattening up). In fact, it was this "feasting" (riches kept for themselves) that had insulated them (like a layer of fat against the cold) from feeling and responding to the needs of others. In a real sense, they were doing just the opposite of what God commanded to be done with their abundant wealth.

In America, this is a lesson we would do well to learn. In the land that flows with not only milk and honey but also storage units filled to the brim with our excess goods, our neighbors are going without!

To the believers Ya'akov is addressing, he says they are to be judged for their actions, much like Cain was judged for his self-centered behavior towards his brother. In fact, the rabbis equate the killing of Abel by his brother, Cain, as being synonymous with "the casting down of the poor and needy."[202]

Is it any wonder then that Ya'akov would choose this story as the backdrop for his lesson on not mistreating one's brother?

---

201 Cp. Genesis 4:4 and James 5:5
202 Midrash Rabbah - Genesis XXII:9 "R. Joshua said in R. Levi's name: It is written, The wicked have drawn out their sword (Ps. XXXVII, 14)-this refers to Cain; To cast down the poor and needy (ib.) refers to Abel;" - Soncino Edition

Finally, what is this "door" that is mentioned in both Genesis and Ya'akov? We will explore this question in our next chapter.

Chapter 18

We ended our last chapter with a cliffhanger. We were just about to discuss what was meant by the phrase "the door" in verse nine. So, let's take a moment and retrace our steps a bit to give some context.

In this final chapter, Ya'akov is reiterating his directions from the beginning of the letter in the traditional Jewish method of instruction. Repeat it, repeat it, repeat it. Repetition seems to be the best way to really learn something. Do it over and over and over until it becomes a part of your life. Well, this is exactly what Ya'akov is doing here at the end of his letter. He's giving them one last warning about getting a handle on their worldly ways of segregating the rich from the poor within their congregations, and squelching the disputes which have arisen because of it.

> **James 5:9 MGI**   Do not murmur against one another, my brothers, so that you should not be judged, for behold, judgment stands before the door.

We started looking at this phrase and found that it was the same imagery that we found in the text of Genesis regarding the first dispute between brothers. I refer to the conversation that God had with Cain after his offering was found unacceptable.

> **Genesis 4:6-7 ESV**   The LORD said to Cain, "Why are you angry, and why has your face fallen? (7) If you do well, will you not be accepted? And if you do not do well, sin is crouching *at the door*. Its desire is for you, but you must rule over it."

181

The ancient rabbis consider this to be one of the five most difficult passages to interpret in all of the Torah.[203] And if, two thousand years ago with one hundred percent accuracy, it was difficult for them to interpret, it would make sense then that as non-Hebrew speaking gentiles living in the culture of the West we might not completely understand it either. Since Ya'akov has been pointing us back to this text as an example, I will attempt to stand on the shoulders of Hebrew scholars from the past to discuss this portion of the passage that we might be able to better apply it to our lives.

> **Genesis 4:6-7 ESV** The LORD said to Cain, "Why are you angry, and why has your face fallen? (7) If you do well, will you not be accepted? And if you do not do well, sin is crouching at the door. Its desire is for you, but you must rule over it."

God had asked for a specific type of sacrifice. Abel brought a bleeding sacrifice to God, whereas Cain brought a bloodless one.[204] Here there's an implied contrast. The implication here is this: since Cain's face had fallen, it is implied that Abel's hadn't. Why is this important? The Hebrew phrase for *"lifting up the countenance"* is connected, not just with the lifting up of one's face but it can also mean: *"to take away, to pardon or take away sin."*[205]

This is why the face is turned up, glad, happy, guilt removed. That state is the result of forgiveness. God is, in effect, asking Cain, *"Do you realize why you have not yet been pardoned of your sins?"*

Then God says:

> **Genesis 4:7b** If you do well, will you not be accepted? And if

---

203   See Babylonian Talmud, Yoma 52a-b

204   Keil & Delitzsch Commentary on the Old Testament, notes on Gen 4:1-8

205   Paul, William. Analysis and critical interpretation of the Hebrew text of the book of Genesis, preceded by a Hebrew grammar, and dissertations on the genuineness of the Pentateuch and on the structure of the Hebrew language. Edinburgh and London: W. Blackwood and sons, 1852 pg. 249

you do not do well, sin is crouching at the door. Its *desire* is for you, but you must *rule* over it.

In my humble opinion, I think the key to understanding what's going on in this verse is found in two Hebrew words used here by God. We find these same two words in a prior discussion God had had with someone else who needed their sins pardoned – her name was Chavah (Eve).

> **Genesis 3:16 ESV**   To the woman he said, "I will surely multiply your pain in childbearing; in pain you shall bring forth children. Your *desire* shall be for your husband, and he shall *rule* over you."

The same words for "desire" and "rule" are repeated in the same order in both the story of Cain and Abel, and in the story of Eve's consequences after her sin.

Just as Eve desired Adam, the sin desired Cain. And just as Eve was subjected to Adam, so the thing crouching at the door must be subjected to Cain. In Hebrew, the thing crouching at the door is called "Chatath Robets." Dr. Adam Clarke reminds us that "*robets is the word used to express the lying down of a quadruped.*"[206]

God says to Cain, in effect: "*You blew it, by not offering an animal sacrifice, but see I've brought you one right here at the door of your tent. Rule over it. (Go kill it!)*" The Hebrew even indicates that this animal was freely offering himself (It's desire is for you).

> **Genesis 4:8 ESV**   Cain spoke to Abel his brother. And when they were in the field, Cain rose up against his brother Abel and killed him.

Rather than offering up the animal that God provided for him, Cain

---

206 Clarke, Adam commentary on the Whole Bible, Genesis 4:7

offers up his brother instead. Why does he take Abel to the field?

> **Genesis 4:3 ESV**   In the course of time Cain brought to the LORD an offering of the fruit of the ground...

It was like Cain was saying to God, *"My brother raises animals, I raise produce. I don't want to sacrifice one of his animals. So, you want a sacrifice of blood? I'll give you a sacrifice of blood!"* And he took his brother Abel to the place where he gathered the offerings which were rejected. And he gave God a sacrifice of blood, that of his brother Abel!

So, when in verse nine, Ya'akov brings up the fighting between brothers and the judgment which waits at the door, he's telling his disciples that, like Cain, God is giving them one more chance. He urges them to listen, and to do the right thing and be forgiven before it's too late!

It's this imagery of the lamb placed before the door of the house that becomes the centerpiece then for the Passover event. The Lamb was to be placed at the door of each person's house, then its blood spilled and placed upon the doorposts.

> **Exodus 12:21-22 ESV**   Then Moses called all the elders of Israel and said to them, "Go and select lambs for yourselves according to your clans, and kill the Passover lamb. (22) Take a bunch of hyssop and dip it in the blood that is in the basin, and touch the lintel and the two doorposts with the blood that is in the basin. None of you shall go out of the door of his house until the morning."

It was on the doorposts that something else would later be placed:

> **Deuteronomy 11:20 ESV**   You shall write them *(the commandments)* on the doorposts of your house and on your gates...

Both the blood and the commandments are to be placed on the

doorposts of one's house. These are clear pictures of the Messiah who is the living Torah and the Lamb of God!

> **Revelation 3:20-21 ESV**   Behold, I stand at the door and knock. If anyone hears my voice and opens the door, I will come in to him and eat with him, and he with me. (21) The one who conquers, I will grant him to sit with me on my throne, as I also conquered and sat down with my Father on his throne.

Today – right now – the same choice is offered. Do we choose to accept the Sacrificial Lamb and His atoning blood? Will we now be obedient to God and follow His instructions for our lives?

Chapter 19

In our last chapter we slowed down and focused on the imagery of "the Door" and the connections between the first story of conflict between brothers and the conflict between the brothers being discussed by Ya'akov.

The brothers had been instructed, re-instructed, warned and now they're being encouraged.

> **James 5:10 MGI** Take the prophets [as] an example, my brothers, for long-suffering with respect to your trials, those who spoke in the name of the LORD.

Once again, Ya'akov is taking his cues from Yeshua at the Sermon on the Mount:

> **Matthew 5:12 ESV** Rejoice and be glad, for your reward is great in heaven, for so they persecuted the prophets who were before you.

This "patience" or "negar rhukha" is something that Ya'akov insists[207] that we have. It's the same phrase that was used in chapter five, verse seven. And if you remember it means: *to possess an enduring spirit.* (I had likened it to how long a person could hold their breath under water.)

The term translated as "trials" is the Aramaic word: "aultsana" and it paints a clear picture for us about what these believers who lived among the gentiles were going through. Aultsana means: "*distress, persecution,*

---

207 In the Aramaic text, this is an imperative verb.

ordeal, torment, tribulation, adversity, affliction, pressure, oppression, trouble, calamity, difficulty, trial."[208]

Little did these believers know that they would have to endure so much in such a short time. It was not long after finishing this letter that Ya'akov himself would be murdered, persecution would rise, and Jerusalem would fall. (Talk about suffering!)

Ya'akov uses the prophets as an example of patience. And now, for his next example of patience, he defers to Job.

> **James 5:11 MGI** For behold, we give a blessing to those who have endured. You have heard of the endurance of Job and have seen the result that the LORD brought to pass for him, because the LORD is merciful and compassionate.

This is probably the best human example of patience in all of scripture. Job suffered with increasingly harder situations and circumstances for months on end.

> **Job 7:3 ESV**   ...so I am allotted months of emptiness, and nights of misery are apportioned to me.

The Jewish commentators view the sufferings of Job like this:

> ... the Jews (p) make them to be twelve months: and these months were "months of vanity", or "empty" (q) ones; such as winter months, empty of all joy, and peace, and comfort; times in which he had no pleasure, no ease of body or of mind; destitute of the good things of life, and of the presence of God and communion with him; and full of trouble, sorrow, and distress: and these were "given him for an inheritance" (r);[209]

---

208 Magiera, "ܐܘܠܨܢܐ " #0103
209 (p) Vid. Misn. Ediot, c. 2. sect. 10. & R. Simeon Bar Tzemach, in loc. (q) יהי

No wonder Ya'akov uses Job as an example. He lost his health, his wife, his family, his money, his belongings, his friends, but not his faith! His faith was planted even deeper by endurance which produced patience.

And this is Ya'akov's point: *"Look at the trials Job went through and how blessed he became after it was all over!"* This, too, is a reiteration of what He taught in chapter one:

> **James 1:4 ESV**   And let steadfastness have its full effect, that you may be perfect and complete, lacking in nothing.

Repeat, repeat, repeat! Repetition is a powerful teaching method.

> **James 5:12 MGI**   Now above everything, my brothers, do not swear, neither by heaven, nor by earth, not even by [any] other oath. But rather, your word should be, "Yes, yes, and no, no," so that you should not be condemned under judgment.

Here again, we find an example of teaching by repetition. Ya'akov has returned again to the subject of speech. And once again, we see that he was certainly influenced by Yeshua's teaching at the Sermon on the Mount.

> **Matthew 5:34-37 ESV**   But I say to you, Do not take an oath at all, either by heaven, for it is the throne of God, (35) or by the earth, for it is his footstool, or by Jerusalem, for it is the city of the great King. (36) And do not take an oath by your head, for you cannot make one hair white or black. (37) Let what you say be simply 'Yes' or 'No'; anything more than this comes from evil.

שוא "menses vacuos," V. L. so Tigurine version, Michaelis. (r) הנהלתי "accepi hereditate", Pagninus, Montanus, Bolducius; so Cocceius, Schmidt, Schultens. As quoted by Gill in Job 7:3

The point being made here can be found in the tradition of taking a vow that is not considered binding because it was not taken "in the name of God," but by using a substitutionary name when referring to God. (Like saying, "I swear by heaven...") And this was the practice of the day. Either way, both Yeshua and Ya'akov are, in effect, saying, *"Don't swear by God, or by the things of God, but just do what you say! Keep your word, or you bring judgment upon yourself!"* When we make a promise in the name of God and then don't keep it, we make people think poorly of Him.

> **James 5:13 MGI**   And if one of you should be in a trial, he should pray, and if he is glad, he should sing psalms.

The verbs here, both "pray" and "sing" are imperfect, which means that these Jews were to make this their ongoing lifestyle. And for the last two thousand years of Jewish history, they have!

The question here is: *How does a person in pain learn to be joyous?* This is accomplished by remembering what the prophets and Job endured and also overcame! This, at least, is the starting point. It is this thought which brings strength along the way. This mindset and focus is the cool water to refresh the weary traveler on an incredibly hot day.

Through out all the sufferings, they continued to pray and they sang psalms! Through the slanders, the burning of their books and the ransacking of their homes and synagogues, they prayed and they sang psalms!

Jews tend to show a bit of levity about their history of persecutions. At any gathering one might easily hear the following remark.

"They Tried To Kill Us. We Survived. Let's Eat!"

Through their heartache, may we as the grafted branch, grow in wisdom and sensitivity toward them as a people. May we find ways to help ease their suffering and pain! And may we prove to be a faithful brother or sister through our faith in the God of Abraham, Isaac and Jacob!

> **James 5:14-15 MGI**   And if one is sick, he should call for the elders of the church and they should pray for him and anoint him [with] oil in the name of our Lord. (15) And the prayer of faith will heal him who is sick and our Lord will raise him, and if [any] sins were committed by him, they will be forgiven.

The practice of the calling of elders takes us back to the story of Moses found in chapter eleven of the book of Numbers. There we find the mixed multitude complaining and once again, as Moses bears the brunt of it. He bears what he calls "an affliction." What is God's remedy for Moses' affliction? Delegation.

> **Numbers 11:16, 24-25 ESV**   Then the LORD said to Moses, "Gather for me seventy men of the elders of Israel, whom you know to be the elders of the people and officers over them, and bring them to the tent of meeting, and let them take their stand there with you..."(24) So Moses went out and told the people the words of the LORD. And he gathered seventy men of the elders of the people and placed them around the tent.   (25) Then the LORD came down in the cloud and spoke to him, and took some of the Spirit that was on him and put it on the seventy elders. And as soon as the Spirit rested on them, they prophesied. But they did not continue doing it.

This temporary affliction of Moses was relieved by the elders standing or uniting with him.

We find that the elders (or older and wiser ones in the congregation) were also to take part in the transfer of the people's sins onto the head of the sacrifice.

Leviticus 4:13-20 ESV   If the whole congregation of Israel sins unintentionally and the thing is hidden from the eyes of the assembly, and they do any one of the things that by the LORD's commandments ought not to be done, and they realize their guilt, (14) when the sin which they have committed becomes known, the assembly shall offer a bull from the herd for a sin offering and bring it in front of the tent of meeting. (15) And the elders of the congregation shall lay their hands on the head of the bull before the LORD, and the bull shall be killed before the LORD. (16) Then the anointed priest shall bring some of the blood of the bull into the tent of meeting, (17) and the priest shall dip his finger in the blood and sprinkle it seven times before the LORD in front of the veil. (18) And he shall put some of the blood on the horns of the altar that is in the tent of the meeting before the LORD, and the rest of the blood he shall pour out at the base of the altar of burnt offering that is at the entrance of the tent of the meeting. (19) And all its fat he shall take from it and burn on the altar. (20) Thus shall he do with the bull. As he did with the bull of the sin offering, so shall he do with this. And the priest shall make atonement for them, and they shall be forgiven.

This same image of standing with someone and offering assistance with the transference of sin is the very imagery Ya'akov conveys here in his letter as he refers to healing of the sick and forgiveness of sins. In the case of the Leviticus passage, it was specifically for the removal of sins only. There is a direct correlation made in the scriptures to sickness and sin, but we would be terribly remiss in our thinking to believe that every persons sickness is always the result of their sin. In Yohanon's gospel, Yeshua is seen healing a man born blind. And the disciples ask Him a question regarding his illness.

John 9:2 ESV   And his disciples asked him, "Rabbi, who sinned, this man or his parents, that he was born blind?"

Consider Yeshua's response:

John 9:3 ESV Jesus answered, "It was not that this man sinned, or his parents, but that the works of God might be displayed in him."

Yeshua makes it clear in His statement that just because a person has an infirmity it doesn't mean that the person's sin has brought it about.

Sickness may ultimately be seen as the result of sin, but that sin takes us all the way back to the garden when man was pronounced with an incurable death sentence as a result of the fall. Ultimately, it is sin that will cause the degradation of these bodies and bring our death.

The practice of the elders anointing the head of the sick and the laying on of hands became a common practice among the Jewish people and in the ancient world.

Scholar John Gill points out the following:

> It was a kind of proverbial saying of Aristophanes the grammarian; the works of young men, the counsels of middle aged persons, and ευχαι γεροντων, "the prayers of ancient men."[210]

We find something similar written in the Mishnah:

> R. Phinehas b. Hama gave the following exposition: Whosoever has a sick person in his house should go to a Sage who will invoke [heavenly] mercy for him; as it is said: "The wrath of a king is as messengers of death, but a wise man will pacify it."[211]

Back to our topic of being anointed for healing, we find this example from the gospel of Mark:

Mark 6:13 ESV And they cast out many demons and anointed

---

210 Apud Harpocratian. Lex. p. 125 as quoted by Gill on James 5:14
211 Mishna, Baba Bathra 116a (Soncino Edition)

with oil many who were sick and healed them.

In my opinion, the anointing of oil, whether on the priest or on the sacrifice was a mark of identification with the Messiah. For "to anoint" is the root meaning of the title Meshiach (Messiah). He is the Anointed One. And He is both the ultimate sacrifice and the priest who offers it up to take away our sin.

> **v.15** And the prayer of faith will heal him who is sick and our Lord will raise him, and if [any] sins were committed by him, they will be forgiven.

These three categories of prayer are still found today in the Jewish prayer called "The Amidah." In fact, it was this same prayer that played a key role in the first century Jewish sect at the Dead Sea. In what's been titled "A Messianic Apocalypse Scroll" the Essenes wrote:

> ...He who liberates the captives, restores sight to the blind, straightens the bent... for He will heal the wounded, and revive the dead and bring good news to the poor...[212]

The ancient prayers and the categories they fall into were influenced heavily by the prayers of David. And Ya'akov, as well as the Essenes, rightfully considered the Messiah as the healer.

Sometimes sickness is actually caused by sin. In this case, by anointing and prayer, just as the sins are transferred from the people to the bull, so the sickness "leaves" the ill person. For that is what the Aramaic word "shevaq," translated as "forgiven," literally means.[213] Shevaq is definitely a vivid picture of the sins of the people being transferred to the sacrifice.

---

212 Vermes, The Complete Dead Sea Scrolls in English, 4Q521 pg. 392

213 Magiera, "ܫܒܩ" #2440

> **James 5:16 MGI** Now confess your faults to one another and pray for one another to be healed, for great is the power of prayer that a just man prays.

The Aramaic term used for "sin" in the case of a person who was sick due to his own sin is "khetaha," which simply indicates "*sin or fault.*"[214] This is the term for those sins which are seen as "leaving."

Here, we have a different word for "sin" or "faults" which is: "saklutha." This Aramaic term means: "*foolishness, transgression, offense, wrong-doing, fault, error.*"[215] And in the same way that the prayer and anointing caused the sickness to "leave" in verse fifteen, so here, the act of "confession" brings healing. Confession, or "yada," means: "*throwing or casting something out.*"[216]

It's important to note that the "healing" that is mentioned in verse sixteen is not a one-time event. It is seen as an ongoing process, where a lifestyle of being foolish is then thrown out so that healing can take place. We are a broken people by default. We are more apt to stumble than to walk upright. And more prone to go astray than to stay on the path. Ya'akov reminds us that it's by the processes that the Messiah established within the assembly, through both the work of the leaders and congregants, that we can find wholeness and healing.

---

214 Magiera, "ܚܛܗܐ" # 0771
215 Ibid., "ܣܟܠܘܬܐ" #1652
216 Ibid., "ܝܕܐ" #1020

Chapter 20

In our last chapter, we explored the imagery and language of the sacrificial system. We discussed the process of the priests when laying hands on the scape goat and the offering up of bulls for the transfer of sin from the people of God. And we observed as Ya'akov drew a parallel between that and this same imagery of elders laying hands with the confession and removal of sins amidst the congregation. Now, we complete our study through the letter of Ya'akov.

> **James 5:17 MGI**   Elijah was also a passionate man like us and he prayed that the rain would not fall on the earth. And it did not fall [for] three years and six months.

We have established that prayer can heal the sick, and is therefore a mighty resource for the believer. Ya'akov sites the example of Elijah and the effectiveness of his prayers to encourage his listeners to pray. This word translated as "passionate" is the Aramaic term: "khashusha." Its primary meaning is: *"to be capable of feeling; sympathetic; passionate.*[217]

Ya'akov says that Elijah was like us. Elijah was angry over the people's idolatry, but he prayed! The Jews whom Ya'akov was writing to were being persecuted, they were enduring terrible hardships, one can only guess that they were angry too. Yet, in the midst of Elijah's deep feelings, he prayed. And this is Ya'akov's advice to us. Pray! Pray that you may have the endurance to withstand the persecution. Pray that you can withstand your brother's prejudice. Pray to withstand your current poverty. Pray that your brothers will be healed from the effects of sin in their lives! Pray, pray, pray!

---

217 Magiera, "ܟ̈ܫܘܫܐ" #0913

There's something interesting about Elijah's prayer, beginning with the fact that there's not much of his prayer found in scripture. As a matter of fact, throughout the stories of Elijah in 1 Kings, you won't even find the phrase "Elijah prayed." Quite a bit is written about the situation he was facing, but very little is recorded about what and how he actually prayed.

Here are the primary scriptures which tell us about Elijah and his prayer life.

> **1 Kings 17:20-22 ESV**   And he cried to the LORD, "O LORD my God, have you brought calamity even upon the widow with whom I sojourn, by killing her son?" (21) Then he stretched himself upon the child three times and cried to the LORD, "O LORD my God, let this child's life come into him again." (22) And the LORD listened to the voice of Elijah. And the life of the child came into him again, and he revived.

> **1 Kings 18:36-38 ESV**   And at the time of the offering of the oblation, Elijah the prophet came near and said, "O LORD, God of Abraham, Isaac, and Israel, let it be known this day that you are God in Israel, and that I am your servant, and that I have done all these things at your word. (37) Answer me, O LORD, answer me, that this people may know that you, O LORD, are God, and that you have turned their hearts back." (38) Then the fire of the LORD fell and consumed the burnt offering and the wood and the stones and the dust, and licked up the water that was in the trench.

These are actually the only two scriptures which say that Elijah prayed.

The key, I believe, as to why Ya'akov used him as an example can be found in the Jewish perspective of Elijah's style of prayer. Here is a statement from a medieval Jewish commentary on the Torah which seems to capture the Jewish insights into Elijah's prayers:

That צַלִּי צְלוֹתֵיהּ, "he prayed his prayer"; and of others, that צְלָאן צְלוֹתִין, "they prayed prayers"[218]

This tells us that the way the Jews understood it, rather than praying rote prayers ("praying prayers") Elijah prayed from the heart ("his prayers.") And the difference can be seen by their results! This ancient perspective concerning Elijah's style of personal prayer can still be seen emphasized within the Jewish faith in the traditional story entitled, "The Shepherd." In the opening paragraph of this story we find the following words:

> What is prayer? It is opening our hearts to God, expressing our overwhelming joy in being His creatures and thanking Him for giving us life. The Mahzor, the High Holiday prayer book, contains many beautiful prayers, some centuries old. But prayers that come from the lips and not the heart are only mumbled words. It is not necessary to pray in Hebrew, or even in a synagogue. A simple song chanted in a field can be equal to the prayers of the most learned rabbi. And infinitely more precious.[219]

This is what was so striking about the prayers of Elijah, that they came from his heart!

The term that Ya'akov uses to describe Elijah's prayer is "tsela."[220] It's an Aramaic term that is only used twice in all the TaNaK. It's found in Ezra 6:10 and in Daniel 6:10. The ancient Paleo-Hebrew letters for this word show a picture of a person laying stretched out on the ground before the great shepherd.[221] This "stretching-out prayer" is the same imagery that we find in chapter seventeen of 1 Kings, which shows Elijah stretched

---

218 Zohar in Exodus folio 4. 2. & in Numbers folio 79. 2, as quoted in Gill.

219 Kimmel, Eric A., Days of Awe – Stories for Rosh Hashanah and Yom Kippur, Puffin Books pg. 32

220 Magiera, "ܨܠܐ" #2106 "(1) incline to, bend, turn aside, waver; (2) seek, intend; (3) Pael: pray, beseech.

221 AHLB "ﬨﬥﬡ" #1403

out over the widow's dead son. And it's through this "stretching out" that the boy is brought back to life. I wonder how many miracles might be seen if we were passionate enough to take the time and energy necessary to "stretch out" before God more often? Elijah's prayers were fervent, desperate, and self-denying. He prayed and God kept it from raining. That's a pretty effective prayer! No wonder Judaism has held Elijah in such high esteem!

> **James 5:18 MGI**   And again he prayed and the heaven gave rain and the earth produced its fruit.

To reiterate, there is actually no mention in scripture of Elijah actually praying. Here's the text:

> **1 Kings 18:42 ESV**   So Ahab went up to eat and to drink. And Elijah went up to the top of Mount Carmel. And he bowed himself down on the earth and put his face between his knees.

Elijah's actions demonstrate a person who is intensely praying. Can people tell by our actions that we are people of prayer?

> **James 5:19 MGI**   My brothers, if one of you errs from the way of truthfulness and someone causes him to repent from his error...

The Greek manuscripts leave out the phrases "the way of truthfulness" and "from his error," so, it's good to be studying from the Aramaic text.[222] Keep in mind that the instruction which follows concerns "brothers" which refers to one who has come to faith and has been brought into the family of God through the Messiah. The term "way of truthfulness" should remind us of being on a journey with God, because that is what this word "aurkha" means. It could be translated just as

---

222   Thanks to Rev. Bauscher's exquisite notes on the Aramaic text of James 5:19 which pointed this out.

easily as "*journey*" here in our text.[223] Our journey is one of knowing the truth, living by that truth, and allowing that truth to set us free.

I think that we often underestimate the power of truth. God is called "the God of truth."[224] The scriptures are characterized as truth.[225] The Messiah calls Himself the truth,[226] and even our unity depends upon the characteristic of truth.[227] And it's truth that sets us free![228]

This "erring" of which Ya'akov speaks is very descriptive. Let's break it down. He uses the term: "teya" which can be translated as: "*to wander, err, stray; forget, disregard, escape notice; deceive, seduce, lead astray, turn away, delude.*"[229]

So, within the word "teya" is not only the act of wandering or straying, but is also that which causes it. Our translation contains the phrase, if "*someone causes him to repent from his error.*" The Aramaic term here translated as "causes him to repent" is "pena" and it means: "*turn back, turn around, return, repent; give back, answer, respond to, convert; restore.*"[230]

A believing brother in the midst of his journey with God can wander off the path of that which is truth. His brother or sister may help bring him back so that he may be restored. And that is what it means to repent – to recognize the truth and turn back to it. The language being used here is very Hebraic. The concept of being on the path and wandering from the path form the very foundation of the language of the Hebrews. Being on the path equals being in fellowship and obedience to God. Wandering from the path equals a breach in the relationship due to

---

223 Magiera, "ﬡﬤﬤﬤﬤ" #0038
224 Isaiah 65:16
225 2 Samuel 7:28
226 John 14:6
227 John 17:17
228 John 8:32
229 Magiera, "ﬡﬤ" #0993
230 Ibid., "ﬡﬤ" #1984

disobedience to God. Coming back to the path equals repentance (teshuva) which is literally *a turning back*.

> **James 5:20 MGI** ...he should know that he who turns back a sinner from the error of his way will give life to his soul from death and will blot out a multitude of his sins. End of the Letter of Ya'akov, the Shaliach.

In our final verse, Ya'akov is using the language and message of the tenth chapter of Proverbs:

> **Proverbs 10:12 ESV** Hatred stirs up strife, but love covers all offenses.

Obviously, this scripture was chosen because it deals specifically with fractured relationships among kinsmen. Notice that "straying from the path" leads "his soul to death." Turning around (making teshuva) and getting back on the path of truth brings life again, and "restores his soul from death."

The concept of a soul dying takes us all the way back to the beginning. This was the promise to the first man should he leave the path, disobey God, and eat from the tree of the knowledge of good and evil. This same verbiage can be found in several places, including Ezekiel:

> **Ezekiel 18:4 ESV** Behold, all souls are mine; the soul of the father as well as the soul of the son is mine: the soul who sins shall die.

> **Ezekiel 18:20a ESV** The soul who sins shall die...

When someone leaves the way of truth his soul (nephesh) dies, but if that person is brought back to the truth, his sins are "covered," literally:

"blotted out, deleted, hidden or canceled."[231]

So much for "Once saved, always saved!" We have choices. God is fully capable of saving us. That is not in question. Human beings have been given a freewill and should a person decide to sever their relationship with God and leave the path of truth, he is choosing death. I can't find one scripture which indicates that a person ever loses his freewill.

There are some serious repercussions to consider here in Ya'akov's illustration. The soul dies, and is restored or returned to life again. It's as if the breath of God can't abide with the one who knowingly chooses sin as a lifestyle. However, like Yom Kippur (The Day of Covering), when a person comes back to the path and re-enters their journey with the God of truth, their sins are canceled, deleted, hidden in Him!

Do you want to save a life? Help bring a brother/sister back to God. Become a means by which their waywardness can be covered, erased and forgiven.

The letter then ends with a simple line...

> **v.20b** ...End of the Letter of Ya'akov, the Shaliach.

Most likely this was used as a simple separator between the Apostolic scriptures.

A "Shaliach" was an ambassador or legal emissary who represented the interests of the One who commissioned him.

It's easy to see why Ya'akov was called haTsaddik (the Righteous)! He lived what he taught. Righteous living was so important to this man that it permeates the only letter we have from him.

---

231 Magiera, "ܐ" #1786

Within just a couple of years after writing this, the holy Ambassador of the Lord was murdered. His body was buried at the foundation of the temple. But, his words live on...

May each of us find the path of truth, and remain steadfast in our pursuit of true faith!

Works cited

Bauscher, Glenn David. The Peshitta Aramaic-English New Testament. 1st ed. [Cambridge, N.Y.?]: Lulu Publishing, 2007. Print.

Benner, Jeff A. The Ancient Hebrew Lexicon Of The Bible. 1st ed. College Station, TX: Virtualbookworm.com Publishing, 2005. Print.

Berkson, William, and Menachem Fisch. Pirke Avot. 1st ed. Philadelphia: Jewish Publication Society, 2010. Print.

Brown, Francis et al. The New Brown, Driver, Briggs, Gesenius Hebrew And English Lexicon. 1st ed. Peabody, Mass: Hendrickson, 1979. Print.

Burer, Michael H, W. Hall Harris, and Daniel B Wallace. NET Bible. 1st ed. [Spokane, Wash.]: Biblical Studies Press, 2009. Print.

Charlesworth, James H. The Old Testament Pseudepigrapha. 1st ed. Garden City, N.Y.: Doubleday, 1983. Print.

Clarke, Adam, and Ralph Earle. Adam Clarke's Commentary On The Bible. 1st ed. Grand Rapids: Baker Book House, 1967. Print.

Edersheim, Alfred. The Life And Times Of Jesus The Messiah. 1st ed. Grand Rapids, Mich.: Christian Classics Ethereal Library, 1999. Print.

Eusebius, and Christian Frederic Crusé. Eusebius' Ecclesiastical History. 1st ed. Peabody, Mass.: Hendrickson Publishers, 1998. Print.

Fausset, A. R, David Brown, and Robert Jamieson. Jamieson, Fausset & Brown's Commentary On The Whole Bible. 1st ed. Grand Rapids, Mich.: Zondervan Pub. House, 1961. Print.

Flood, Gavin D. An Introduction To Hinduism. 1st ed. New York, NY: Cambridge University Press, 1996. Print.

Freedman, H, and Maurice Simon. Midrash Rabbah. 1st ed. London: Soncino Press, 1983. Print.

Friberg, Barbara, Timothy Friberg, and Kurt Aland. Analytical Greek New Testament. 1st ed. Grand Rapids, Mich.: Baker Book House, 1981. Print.

Fruchtenbaum, Arnold G. The Messianic Jewish Epistles. 1st ed. Tustin, CA:

Ariel Ministries, 2005. Print.

Gill, John. An Exposition Of The New Testament. 1st ed. London: Printed for George Keith, 1774. Print.

Gill, John. An Exposition Of The Old Testament. 1st ed. London: Printed for the author, 1763. Print.

Gwilliam, George H. The Fourfold Holy Gospel : In The Peshitta Syrac Version =. 1st ed. London: British and Foreign Soc., 1914. Print.

Harris, J. Rendel. The Odes And Psalms Of Solomon. 1st ed. Cambridge [England]: University Press, 1909. Print.

Harris, R. Laird, Gleason L Archer, and Bruce K Waltke. Theological Wordbook Of The Old Testament. 1st ed. Chicago: Moody Press, 1980. Print.

Isidore, and Priscilla Throop. Isidore Of Seville's Etymologies. 1st ed. Charlotte, Vt.: MedievalMS, 2005. Print.

Jenni, Ernst, and Claus Westermann. Theological Lexicon Of The Old Testament. 1st ed. Peabody, Mass.: Hendrickson Publishers, 1997. Print.

Jennings, William, and Ulric Gantillon. Lexicon To The Syriac New Testament (Peshiṭta). 1st ed. Oxford: at the Clarendon Press, 1926. Print.

Jerome, and Thomas P Halton. On Illustrious Men. 1st ed. Washington, D.C.: Catholic University of America Press, 1999. Print.

Josephus, Flavius, William Whiston, and Charles F Pfeiffer. The Works Of Flavius Josephus. 1st ed. Grand Rapids, Mich.: Baker Book House, 1974. Print.

Keil, Carl Friedrich, and Franz Delitzsch. Biblical Commentary On The Old Testament. 1st ed. [Grand Rapids]: [Eerdmans]. Print.

Kimmel, Eric A, and Erika Weihs. Days Of Awe. 1st ed. New York, N.Y., U.S.A.: Viking, 1991. Print.

Kister, Menahem. Avot De-R. Natan. 1st ed. [Israel: ḥ. mo. l., 1993. Print.

Kugler, Robert A. The Testaments Of The Twelve Patriarchs. 1st ed. Sheffield, England: Sheffield Academic Press, 2001. Print.

Lamsa, George M. The Holy Bible From The Ancient Eastern Text. 1st ed. San Francisco: Harper & Row, 1985. Print.

Levine, Amy-Jill, and Marc Zvi Brettler. The Jewish Annotated New

Testament. 1st ed. Oxford: Oxford University Press, 2011. Print.

Magiera, Janet. Aramaic Peshitta New Testament Translation. 1st ed. Truth or Consequences, NM: Light of the Word Ministry, 2006. Print.

Matt, Daniel C. The Zohar. 1st ed. Stanford, CA: Stanford University Press, 2004. Print.

Norton, David. The New Cambridge Paragraph Bible With The Apocrypha. 1st ed. Cambridge: Cambridge University Press, 2005. Print.

Orr, James. The International Standard Bible Encyclopedia. 1st ed. Grand Rapids: W.B. Eerdmans Pub. Co., 1939. Print.

Payne Smith, R, and Jessie Payne Smith Margoliouth. A Compendious Syriac Dictionary. 1st ed. Oxford: Clarendon Press, 1957. Print.

Payne Smith, R, and Jessie Payne Smith Margoliouth. A Compendious Syriac Dictionary. 1st ed. Oxford: Clarendon Press, 1957. Print.

Plumptre, E. H. The General Epistle Of St. James. 1st ed. Cambridge: University Press, 1915. Print.

Roth, Andrew Gabriel. Aramaic English New Testament. 1st ed. Bellingham, Wash.: Netzari Press, 2009. Print.

Santala, Risto. The Messiah In The New Testament In The Light Of Rabbinical Writings. 1st ed. Jerusalem: Keren Ahvah Meshihit, 1992. Print.

Schefzyk, Jürgen. Bibleworks For Windows. 1st ed. Big Fork, Mont.: Hermeneutika, 1997. Print.

Seekins, Frank T. Hebrew Word Pictures. 1st ed. Phoenix, AZ: Living Word Picturs, 2002. Print.

Smith, Jerome H. The New Treasury Of Scripture Knowledge. 1st ed. Nashville, Tenn.: T. Nelson Publishers, 1992. Print.

Spicq, Ceslas, and James D Ernest. Theological Lexicon Of The New Testament. 1st ed. Peabody, Mass.: Hendrickson, 1994. Print.

Stern, David H. Jewish New Testament Commentary. 1st ed. Clarksville, Md.: Jewish New Testament Publications, 1992. Print.

Strong, James, James Strong, and James Strong. The Exhaustive Concordance Of The Bible. 1st ed. Peabody, Mass.: Hendrickson Publishers, 1990. Print.

Talmud. English.,. The Babylonian Talmud. 1st ed. London: Soncino Press,

1935. Print.

Thackston, W. M. Introduction To Syriac. 1st ed. Bethesda, Md.: IBEX Publishers, 1999. Print.

Thayer, Joseph Henry, Carl Ludwig Wilibald Grimm, and Christian Gottlob Wilke. Thayer's Greek-English Lexicon Of The New Testament. 1st ed. Peabody, Mass.: Hendrickson, 1996. Print.

Thigpen, Thomas Paul, and Dave Armstrong. The New American Bible. 1st ed. Huntington, Indiana: Our Sunday Visitor, Inc., 2011. Print.

Tigay, Jeffrey H. Deuteronomy =. 1st ed. Philadelphia [etc.]: Jewish Publication Society, 1996. Print.

Urbino, Solomon b. Abraham b. Solomon d'. Ohel Moed. 1st ed. Wien: G. Brög, 1881. Print.

Vermès, Géza. The Complete Dead Sea Scrolls In English. 1st ed. New York, N.Y., U.S.A.: Allen Lane/Penguin Press, 1997. Print.

Wescott, Brooke Foss, and Fenton John Anthony Hort. The New Testament In The Original Greek. 1st ed. New York: American Book Co. Print.

Zodhiates, Spiros. The Complete Word Study Dictionary. 1st ed. Chattanooga, TN: AMG Publishers, 1994. Print.

CPSIA information can be obtained
at www.ICGtesting.com
Printed in the USA
BVHW011226130720
583611BV00005B/61/J